A clear and obvious track is followed towards Ling Gill (Day 8)

THE PENNINE WAY

This map booklet shows the 426km (265 mile) Pennine Way. This National Trail is Britain's oldest, toughest and best-known long-distance footpath. It stretches from Edale in the Derbyshire Peak District to Kirk Yetholm in the Scottish Borders and can be completed in 2–3 weeks.

Contents and using this guide

This booklet of Ordnance Survey® 1:25,000 Explorer maps has been designed for convenient use on the trail and includes:
- a key to map pages (pages 4–5) showing where to find the maps for each stage
- the full and up-to-date line of the National Trail
- an extract from the OS Explorer map legend (pages 129–131).

In addition, the *Pennine Way* guidebook describes the full route from south to north alongside all you need to know to plan a successful trip and lots of incidental information about local history, geography and wildlife.

Note that the route described in this map booklet is the actual route walked by the author. The route marked 'Pennine Way' on the Ordnance Survey maps differs slightly from the on-the-ground reality.

© Cicerone Press 2025
Second edition 2025
ISBN-13: 978 1 78631 141 2
First edition 2017
Photos © Paddy Dillon 2017

© Crown copyright and
database rights 2025
OS AC0000810376

Cicerone's EU representative for GPSR compliance is Easy Access System Europe, Mustamäe tee 50, 10621 Tallinn, Estonia. Email gpsr.requests@easproject.com.

PENNINE WAY

Day 1	Edale to Torside	7
Day 2	Torside to Standedge	13
Day 3	Standedge to Callis Bridge or Hebden Bridge	19
Day 4	Callis Bridge or Hebden Bridge to Ickornshaw	25
Day 5	Ickornshaw to Gargrave	30
Day 6	Gargrave to Malham	37
Day 7	Malham to Horton in Ribblesdale	38
Day 8	Horton in Ribblesdale to Hawes	44
Day 9	Hawes to Keld	53
Day 10	Keld to Baldersdale or Bowes	56
Day 11	Baldersdale or Bowes to Middleton-in-Teesdale	67
Day 12	Middleton-in-Teesdale to Langdon Beck	68
Day 13	Langdon Beck to Dufton	73
Day 14	Dufton to Alston	78
Day 15	Alston to Greenhead	86
Day 16	Greenhead to Housesteads	94
Day 17	Housesteads to Bellingham	101
Day 18	Bellingham to Byrness	107
Day 19	Byrness to Clennell Street	115
Day 20	Clennell Street to Kirk Yetholm	122

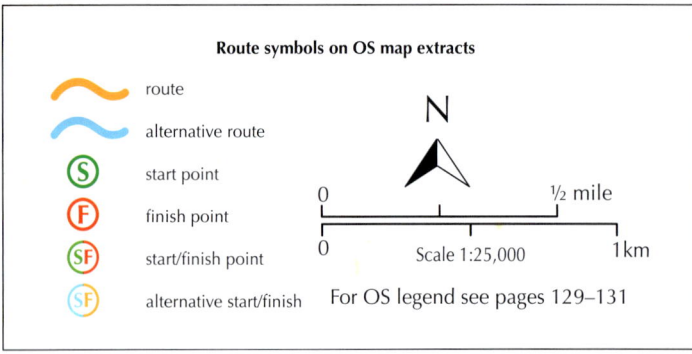

Looking across a meadow to Low Way Farm near Holwick (Stage 12)

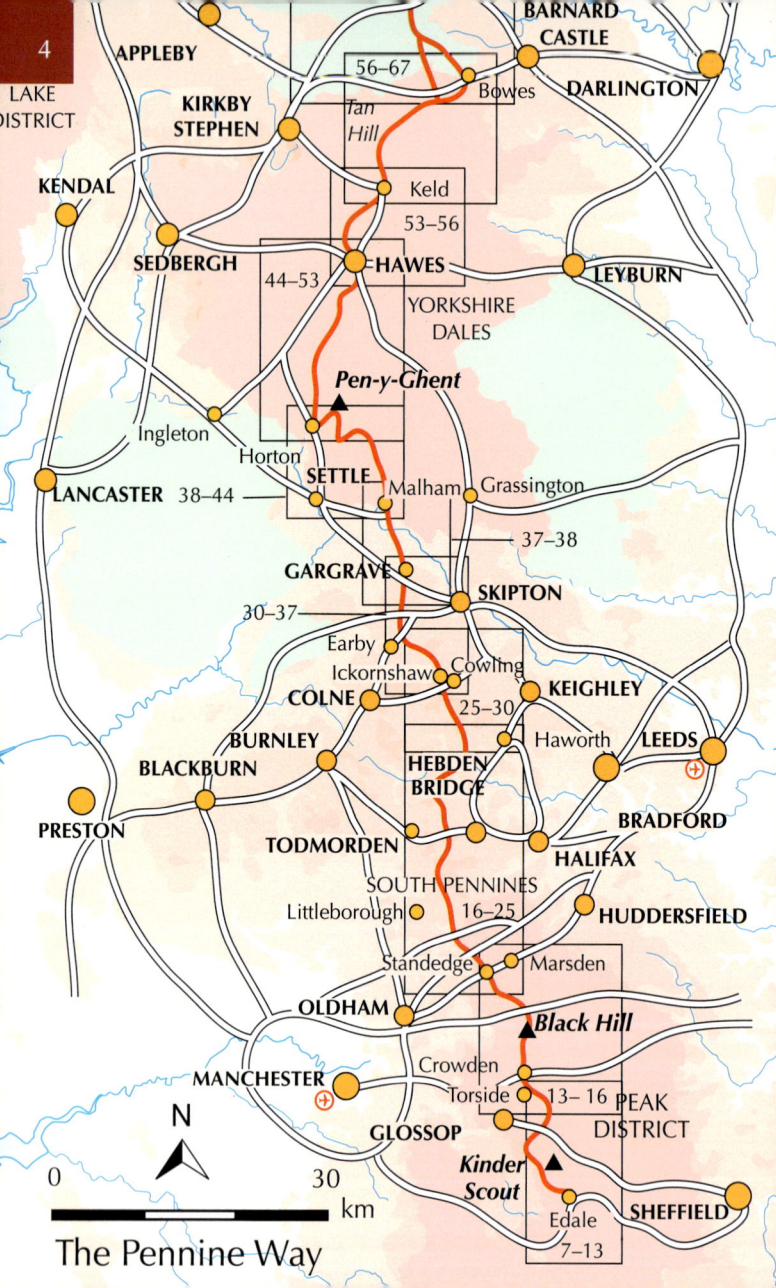

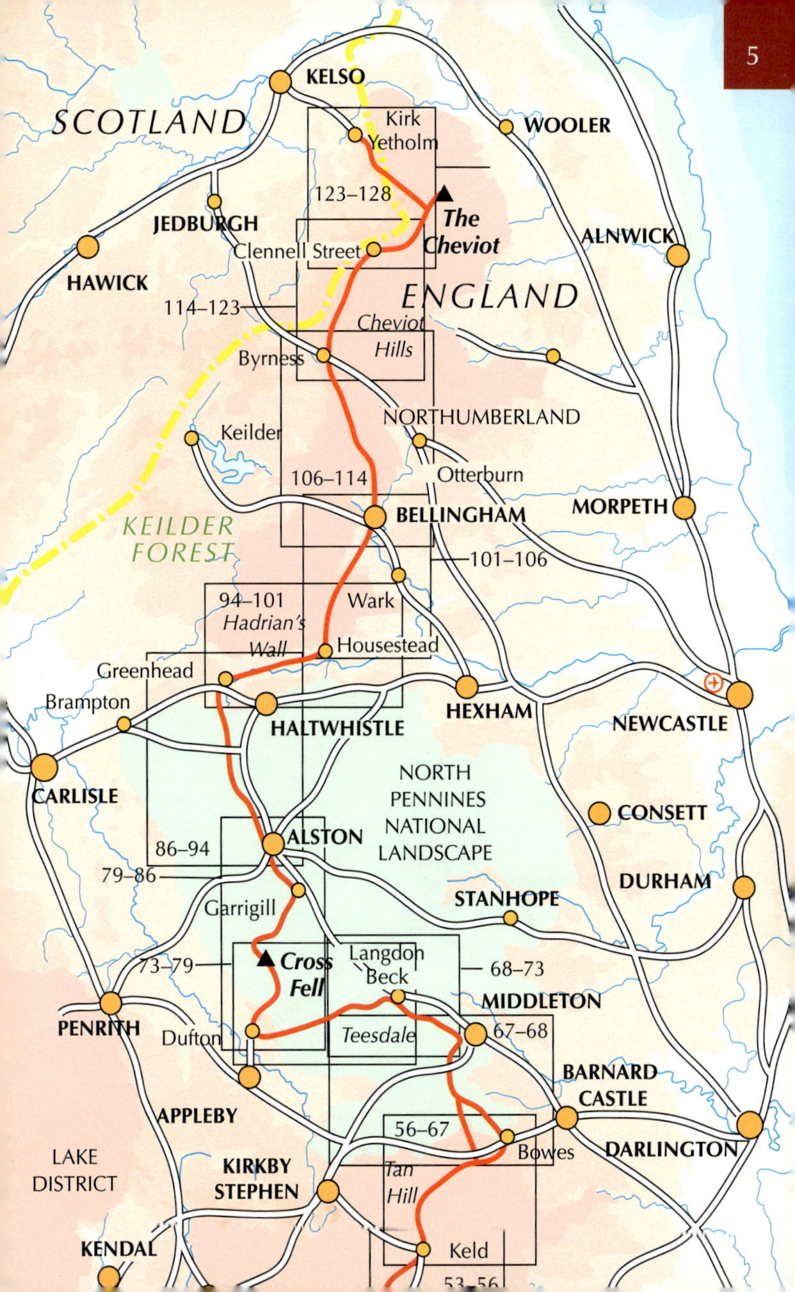

5

SCOTLAND

KELSO
Kirk Yetholm
WOOLER
JEDBURGH
123–128
ALNWICK
HAWICK
Clennell Street
The Cheviot
ENGLAND
114–123
Cheviot Hills
Byrness
Keilder
NORTHUMBERLAND
106–114
Otterburn
MORPETH
KEILDER FOREST
BELLINGHAM
101–106
94–101
Wark
Hadrian's Wall
Housestead
Greenhead
Brampton
HALTWHISTLE
HEXHAM
NEWCASTLE
CARLISLE
NORTH PENNINES NATIONAL LANDSCAPE
CONSETT
ALSTON
86–94
STANHOPE
DURHAM
79–86
Garrigill
73–79
Cross Fell
Langdon Beck
68–73
MIDDLETON
Dufton
Teesdale
67–68
PENRITH
BARNARD CASTLE
APPLEBY
56–67
DARLINGTON
LAKE DISTRICT
KIRKBY STEPHEN
Bowes
Tan Hill
KENDAL
Keld
53–56

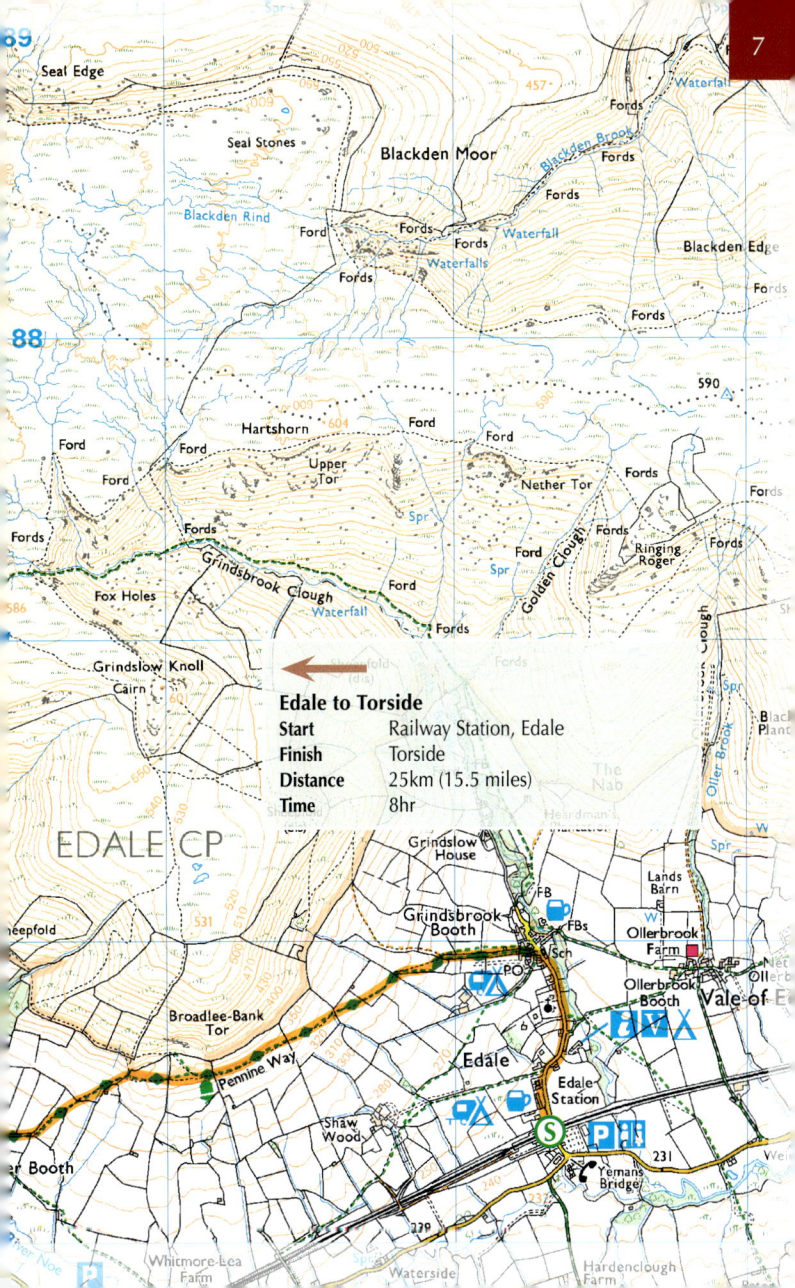

Edale to Torside
Start   Railway Station, Edale
Finish   Torside
Distance 25km (15.5 miles)
Time   8hr

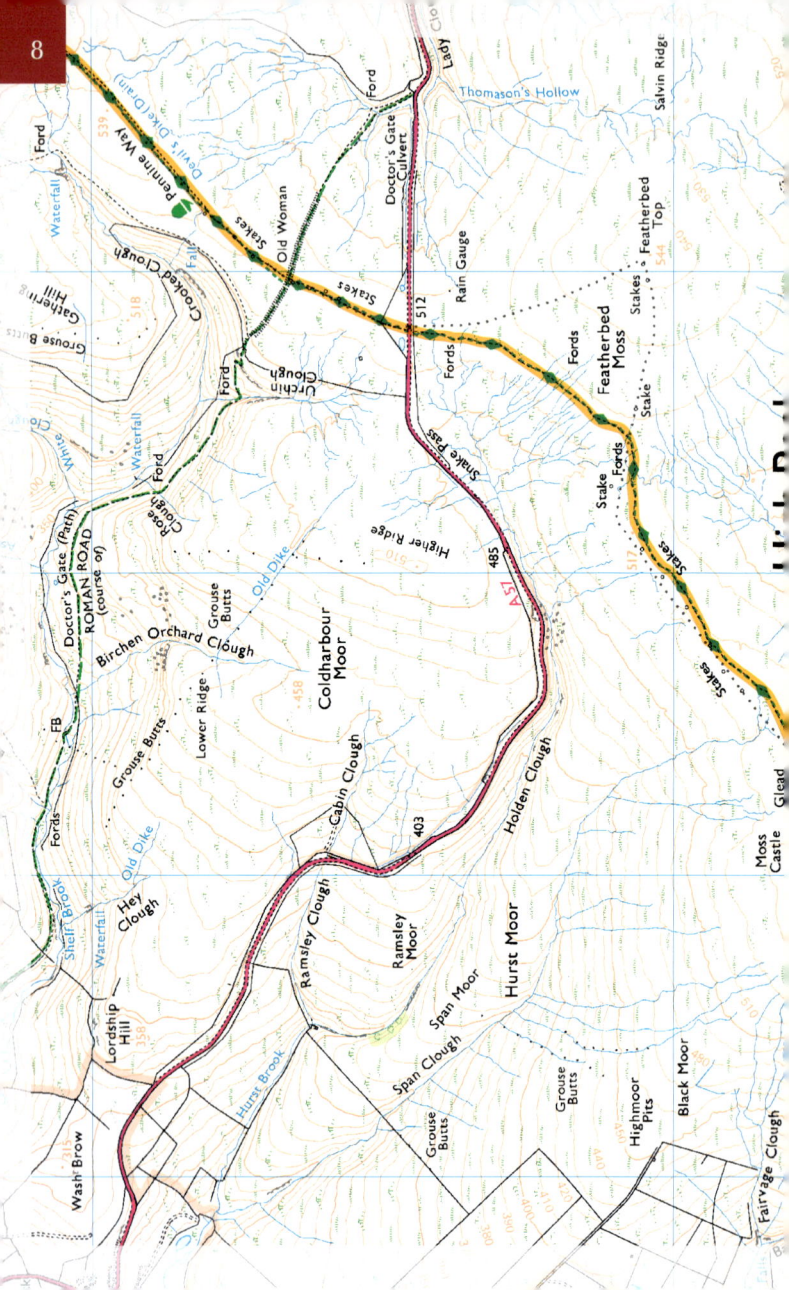

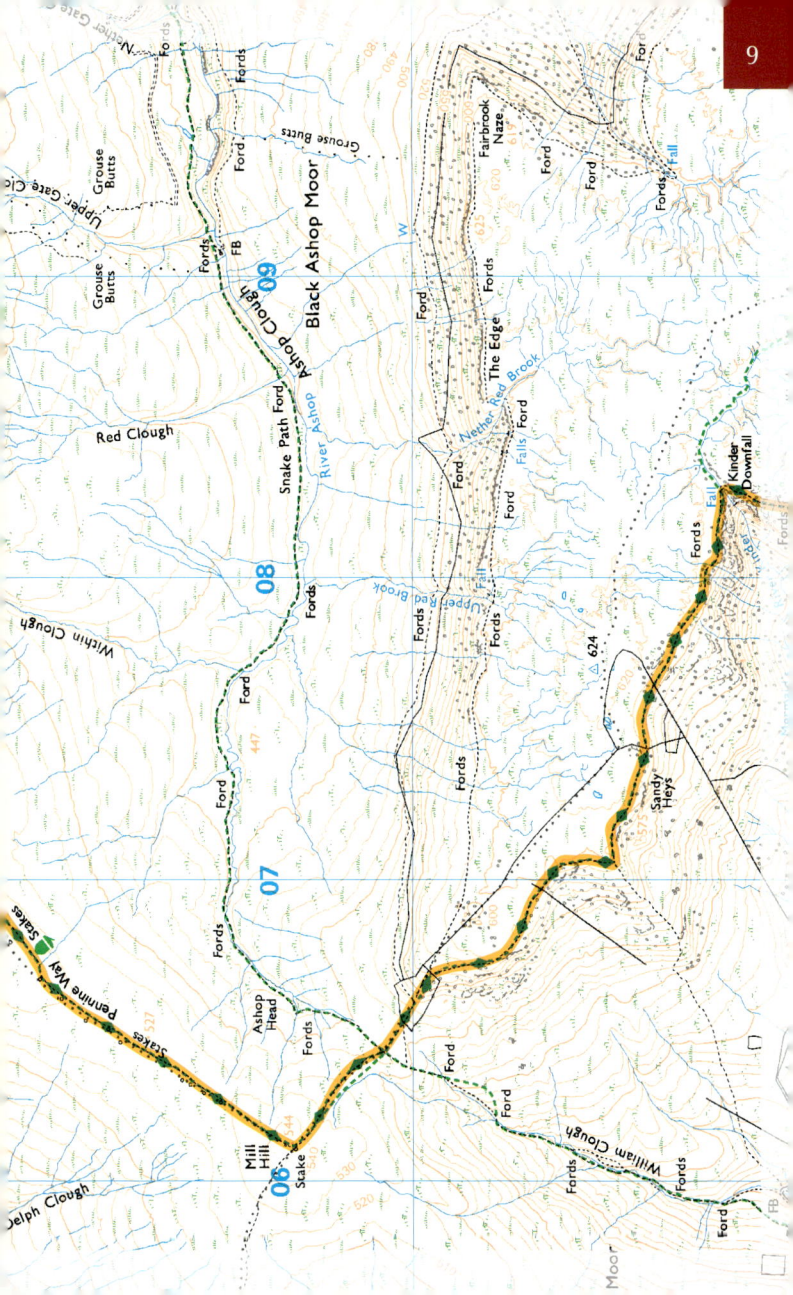

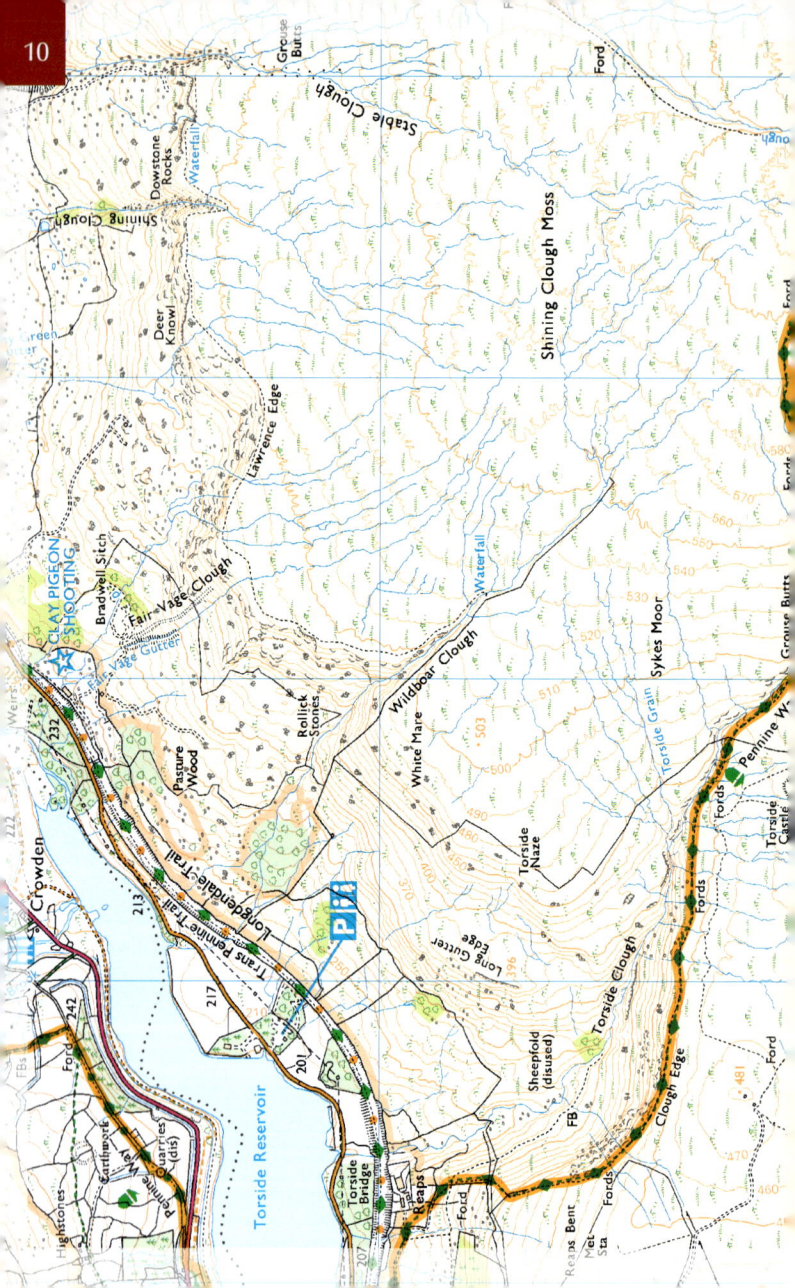

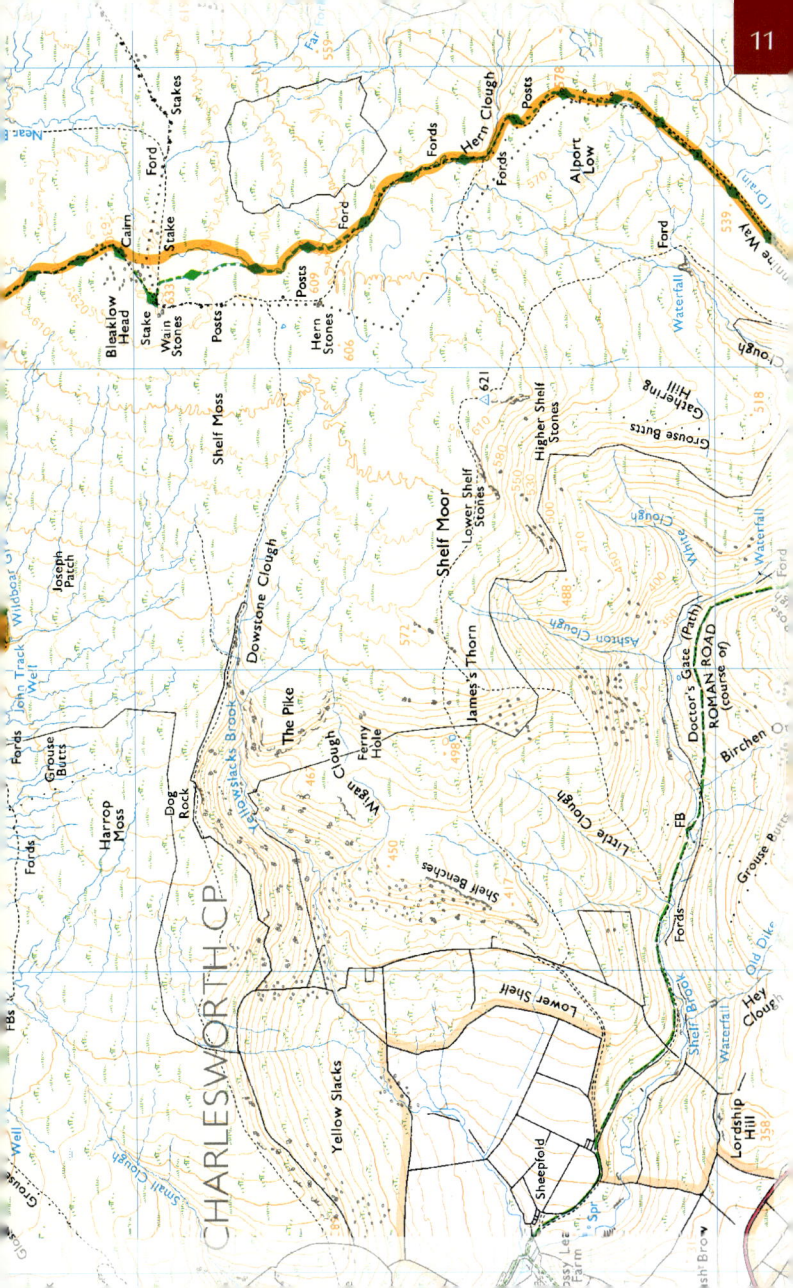

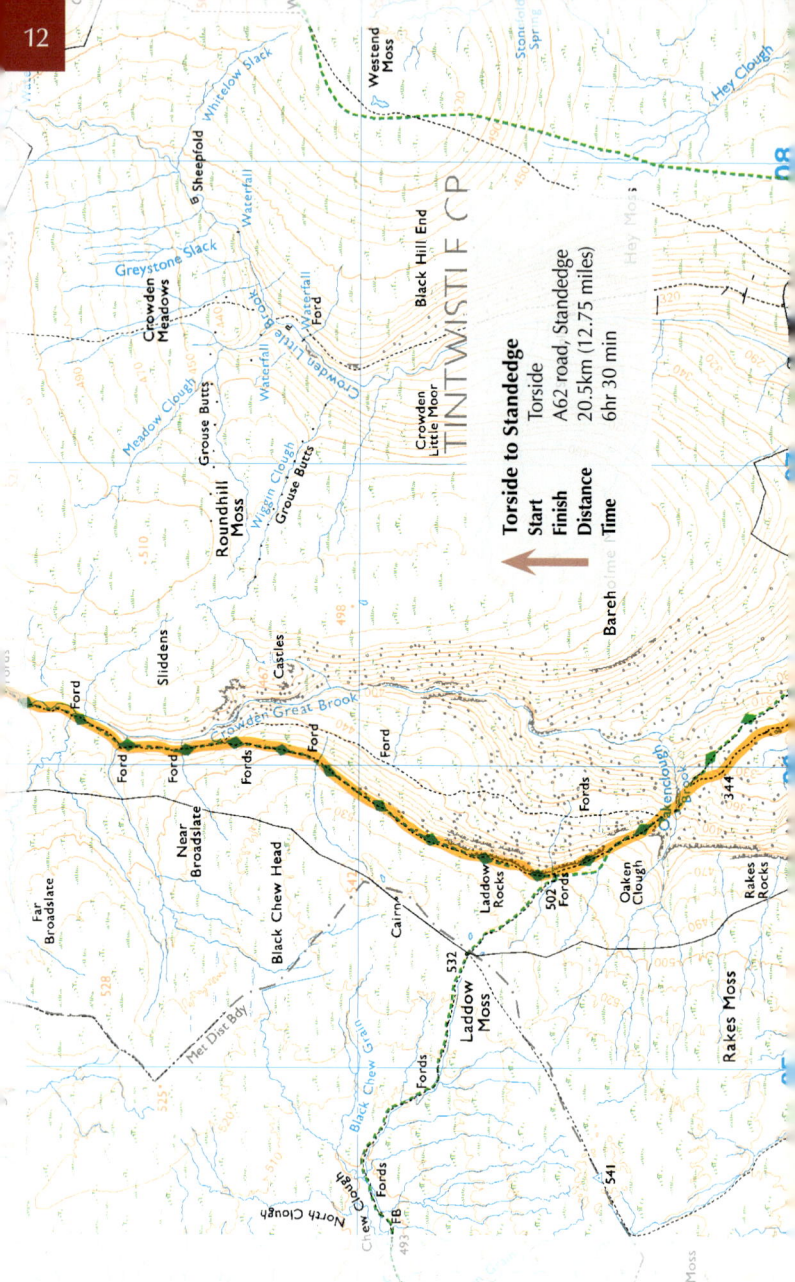

Torside to Edale

Start	Torside
Finish	Railway Station, Edale
Distance	25km (15.5 miles)
Time	8hr

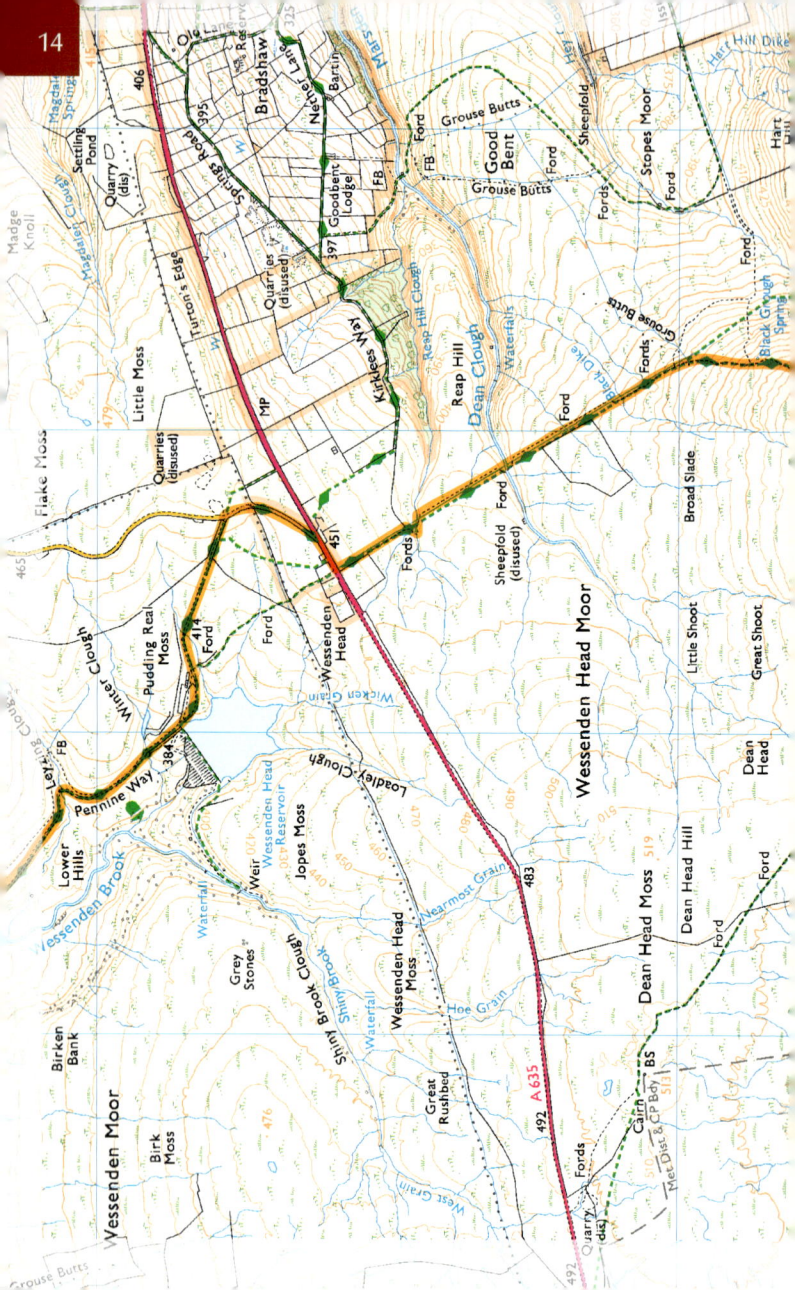

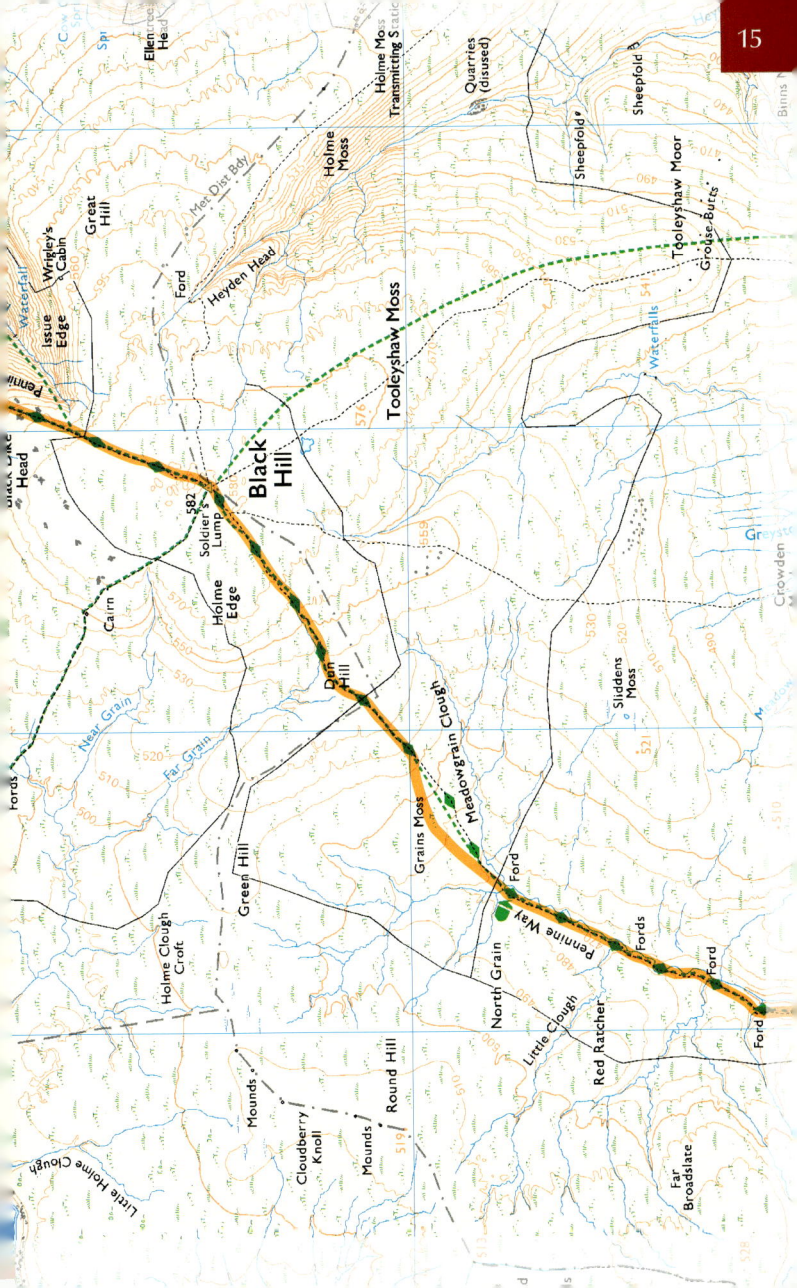

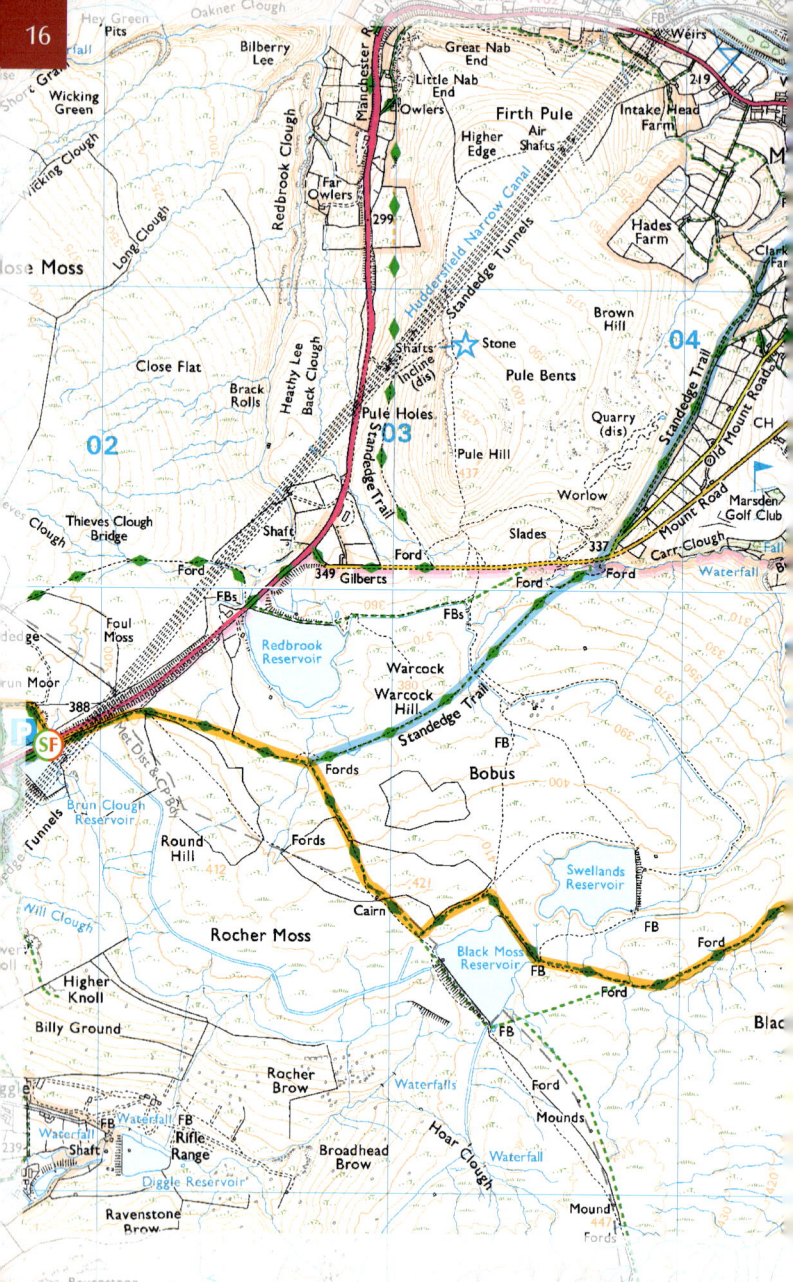

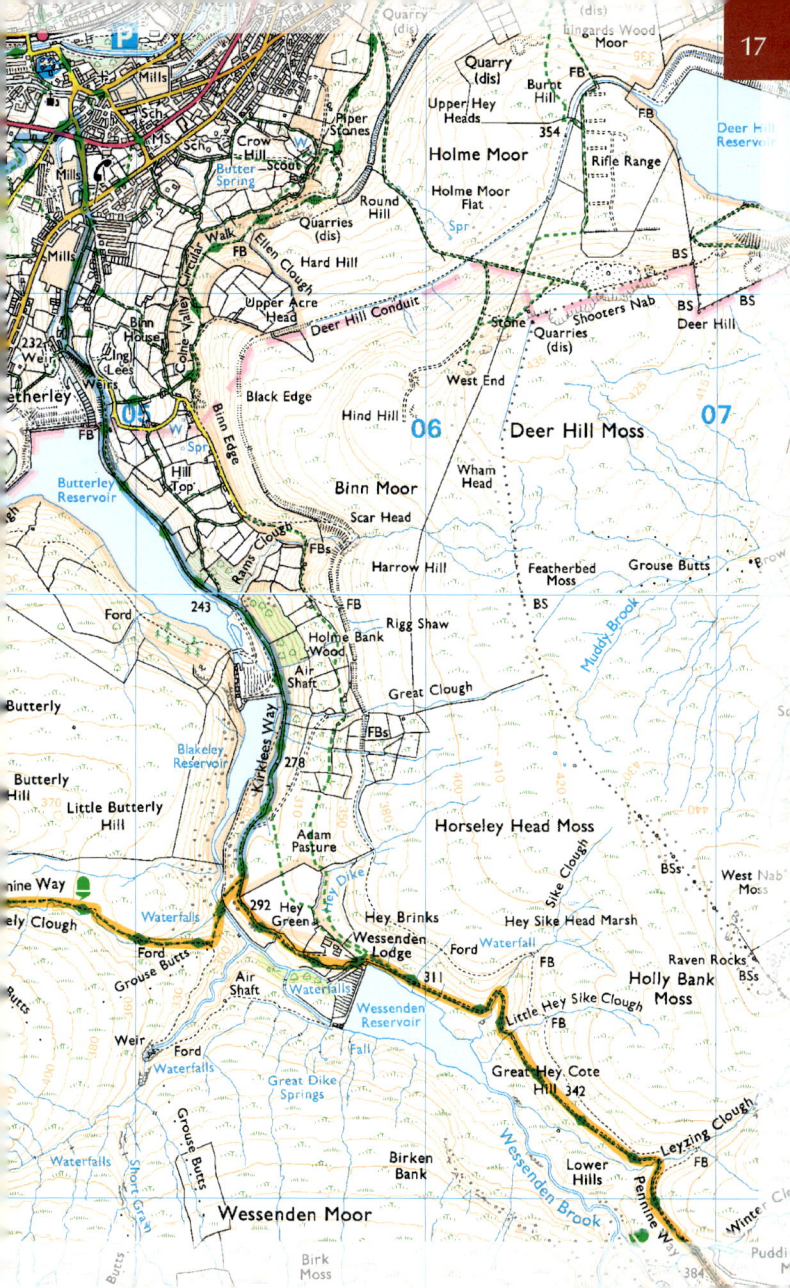

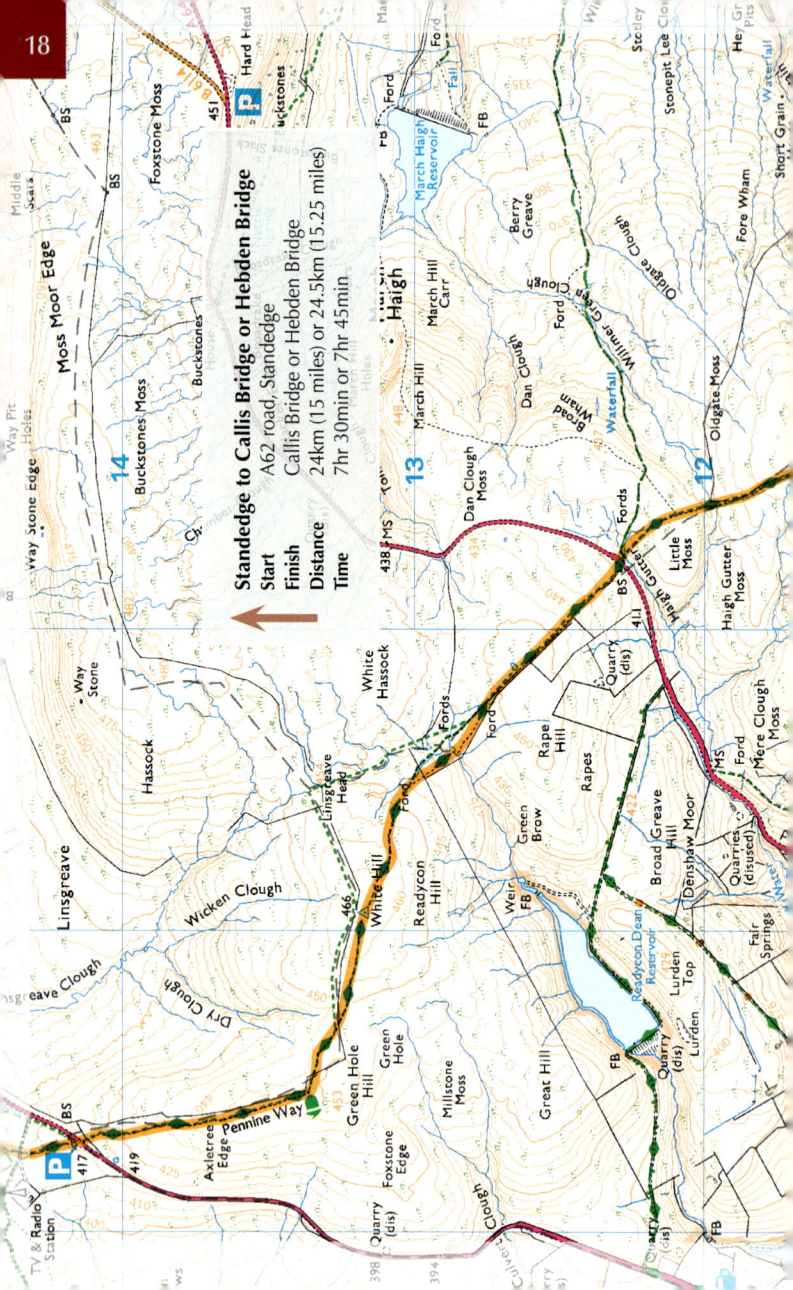

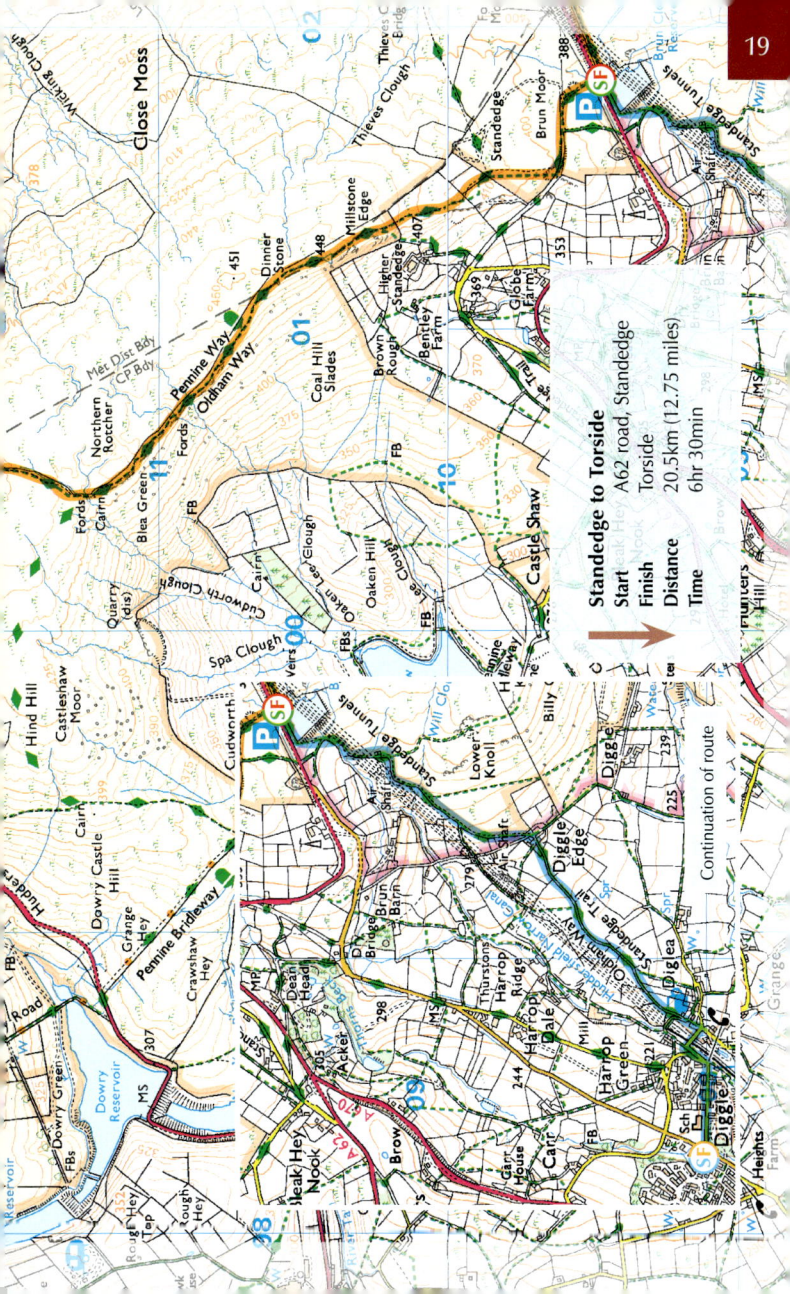

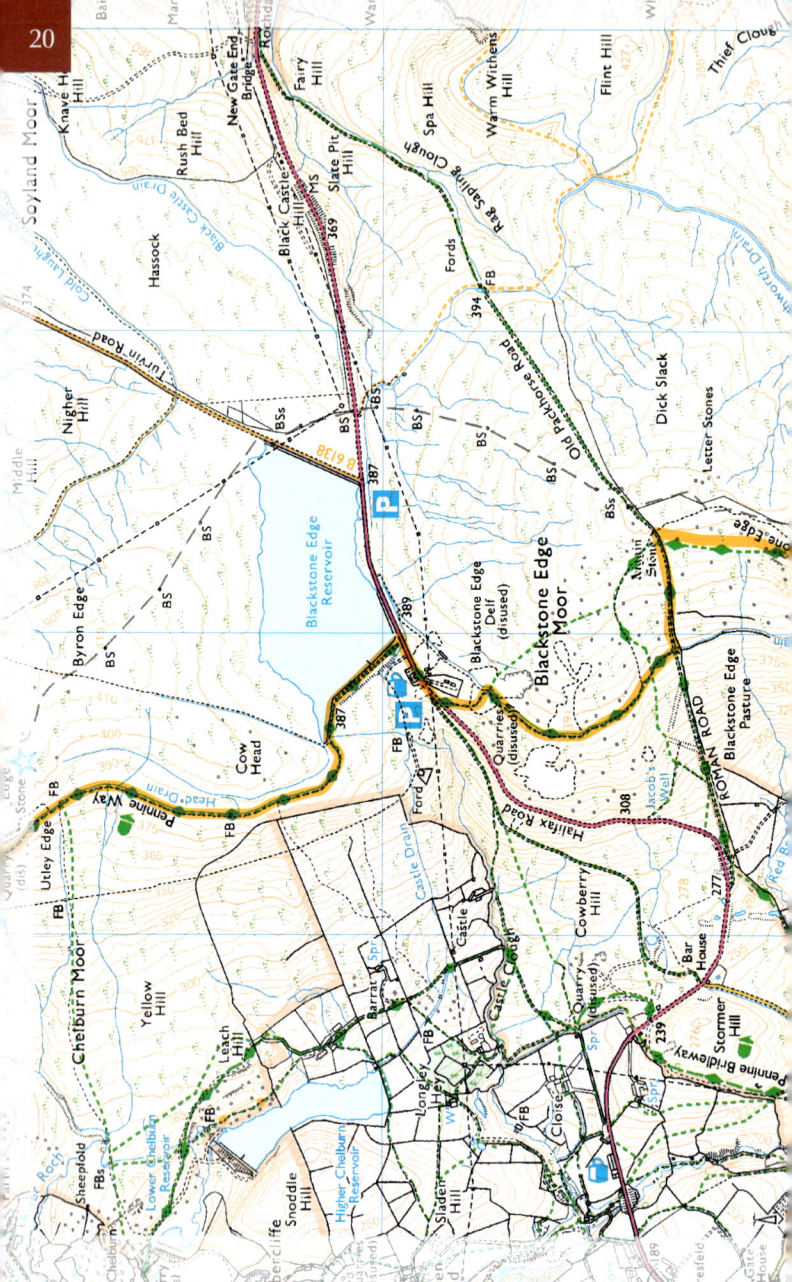

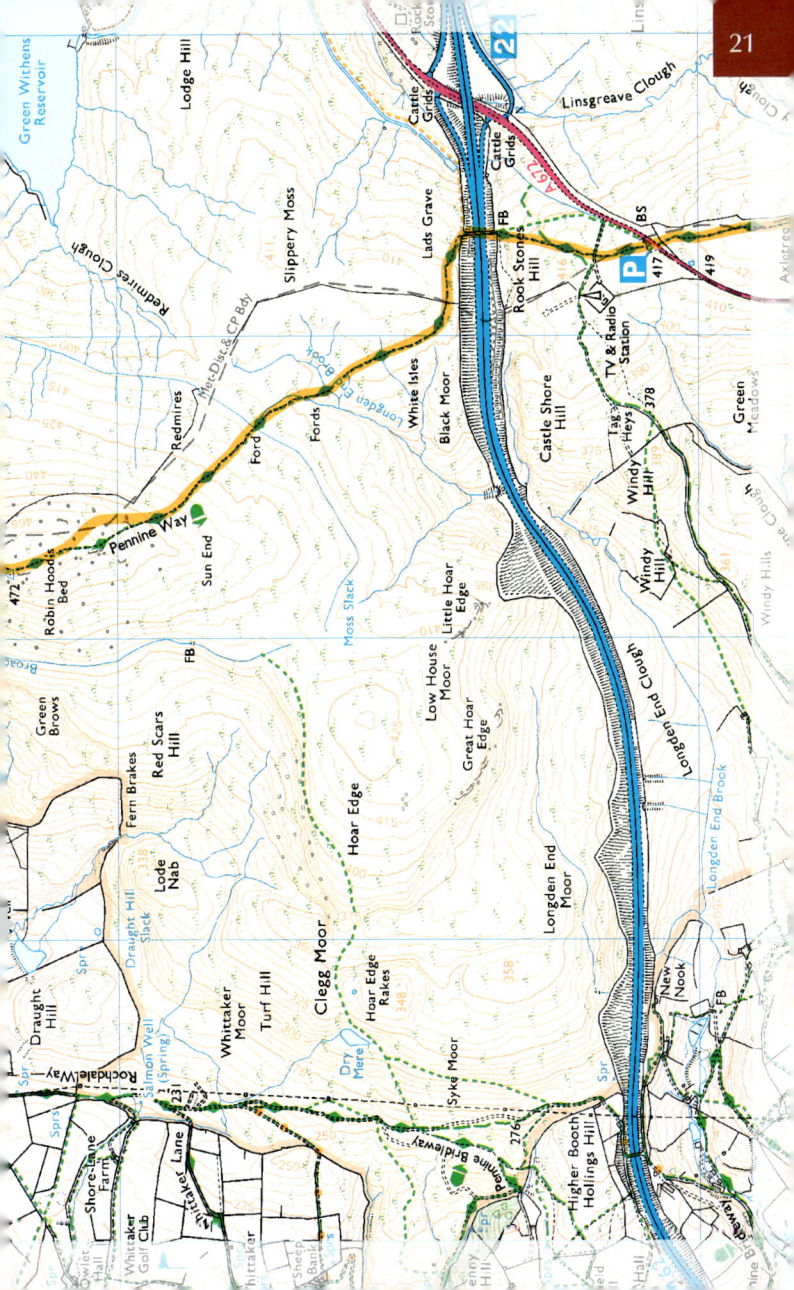

22

24

Callis Bridge or Hebden Bridge to Ickornshaw

Name	Callis Bridge or Hebden Bridge
Start	A6068, Ickornshaw, Cowling
Finish	
Distance	25.5km (16 miles) or 27km (17 miles)
Time	8hr or 8hr 30min

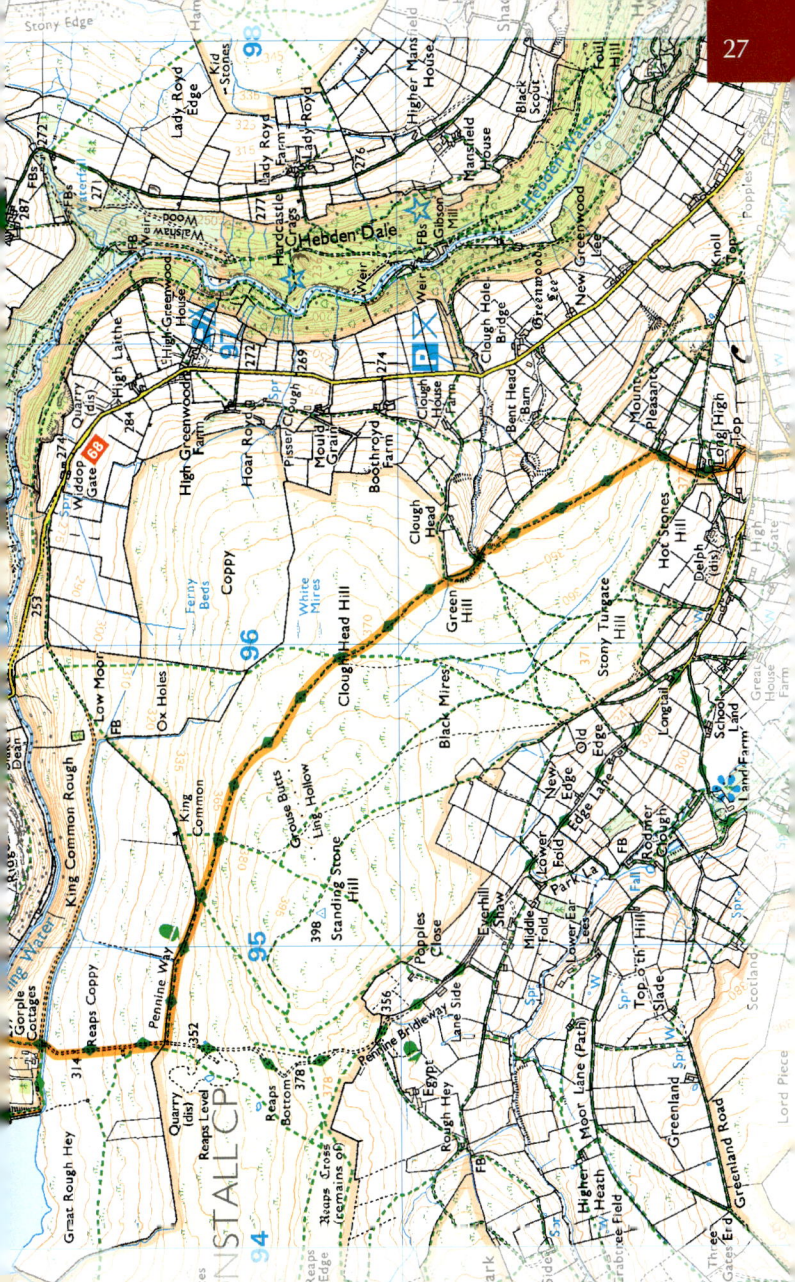

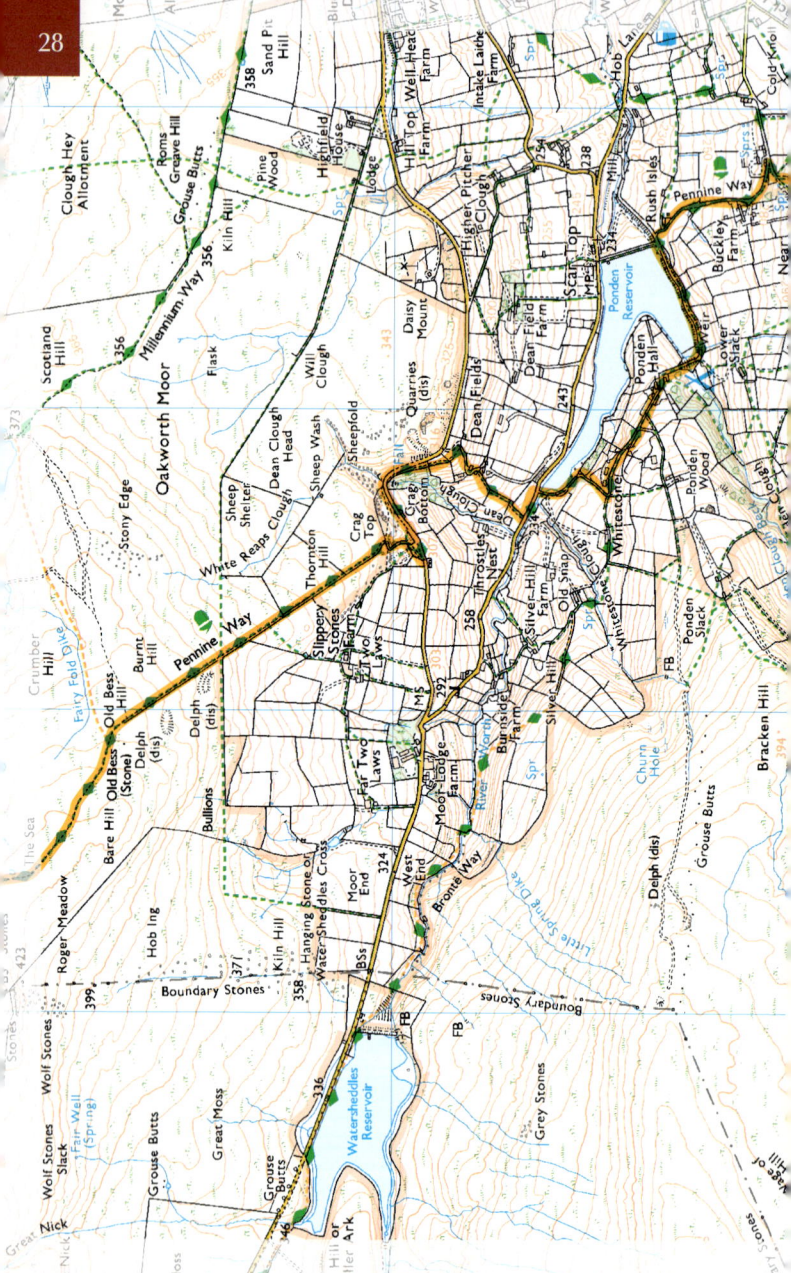

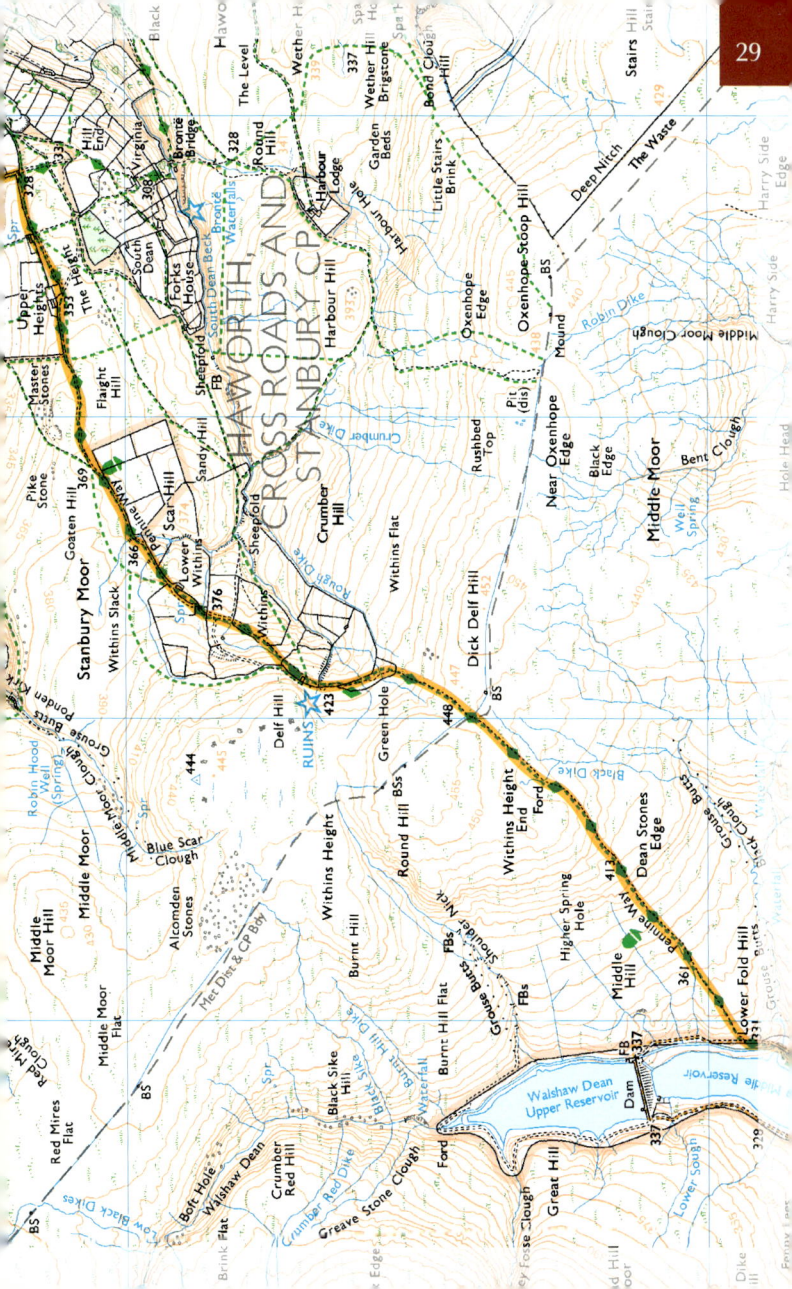

Ickornshaw to Gargrave

Name	A6068, Ickornshaw, Cowling
Start	Ickornshaw
Finish	Dalesman Café, Gargrave
Distance	18km (11 miles)
Time	5hr 30min

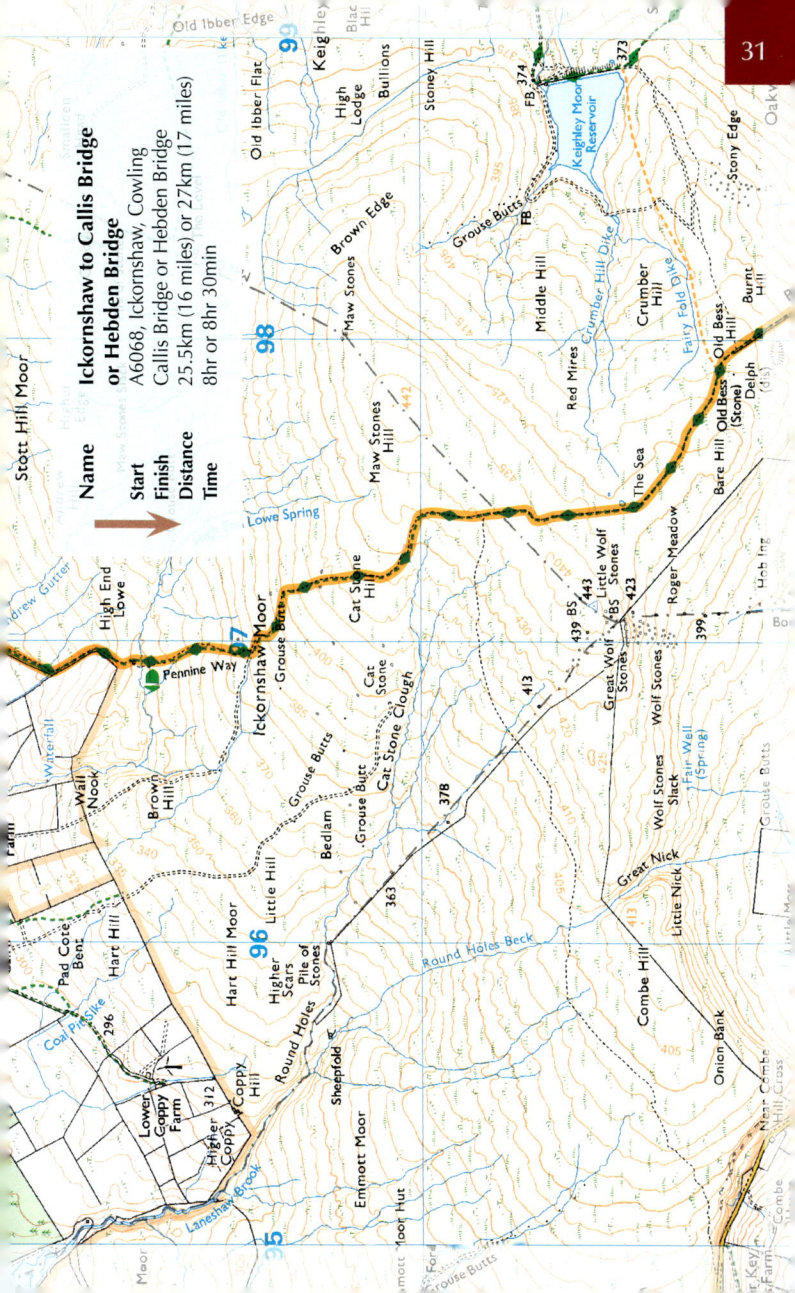

34

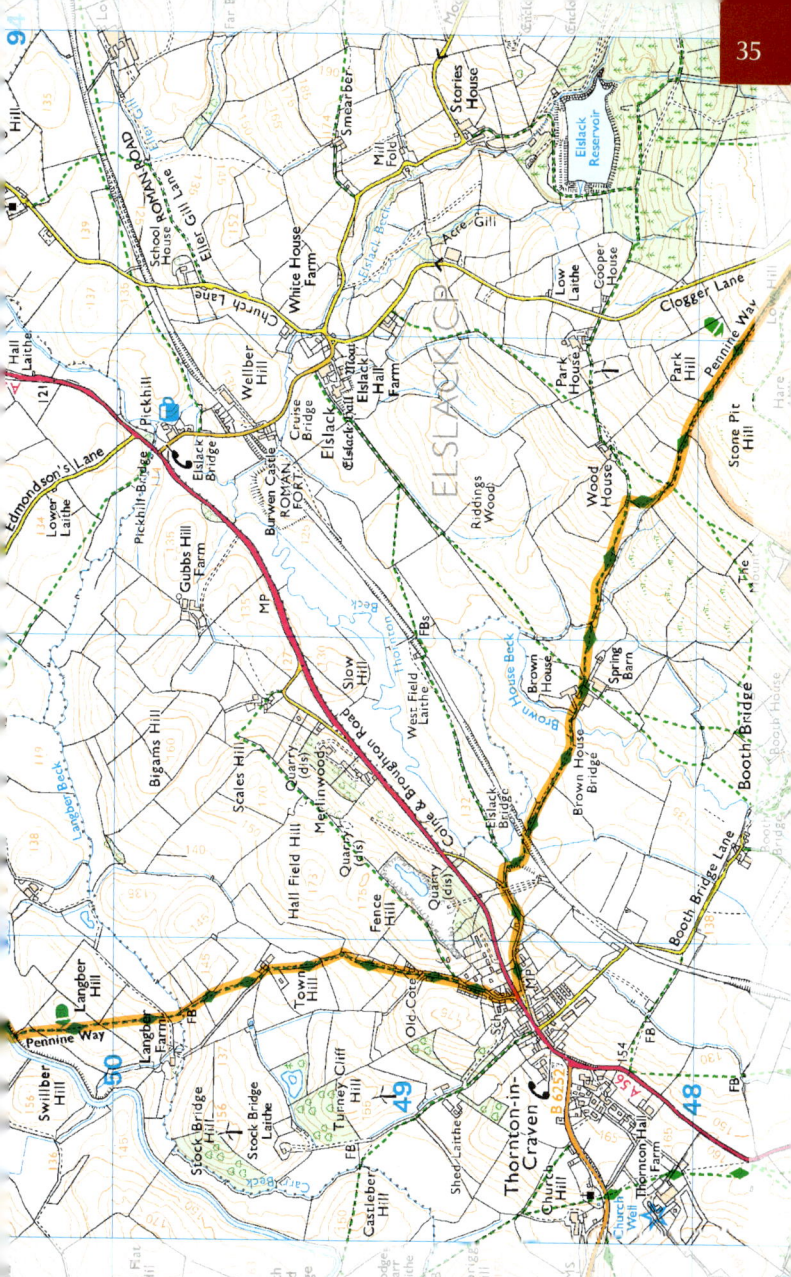

Name	Gargrave to Malham
Start	Dalesman Café, Gargrave
Finish	The Green, Malham
Distance	10.5km (6.5 miles)
Time	3hr

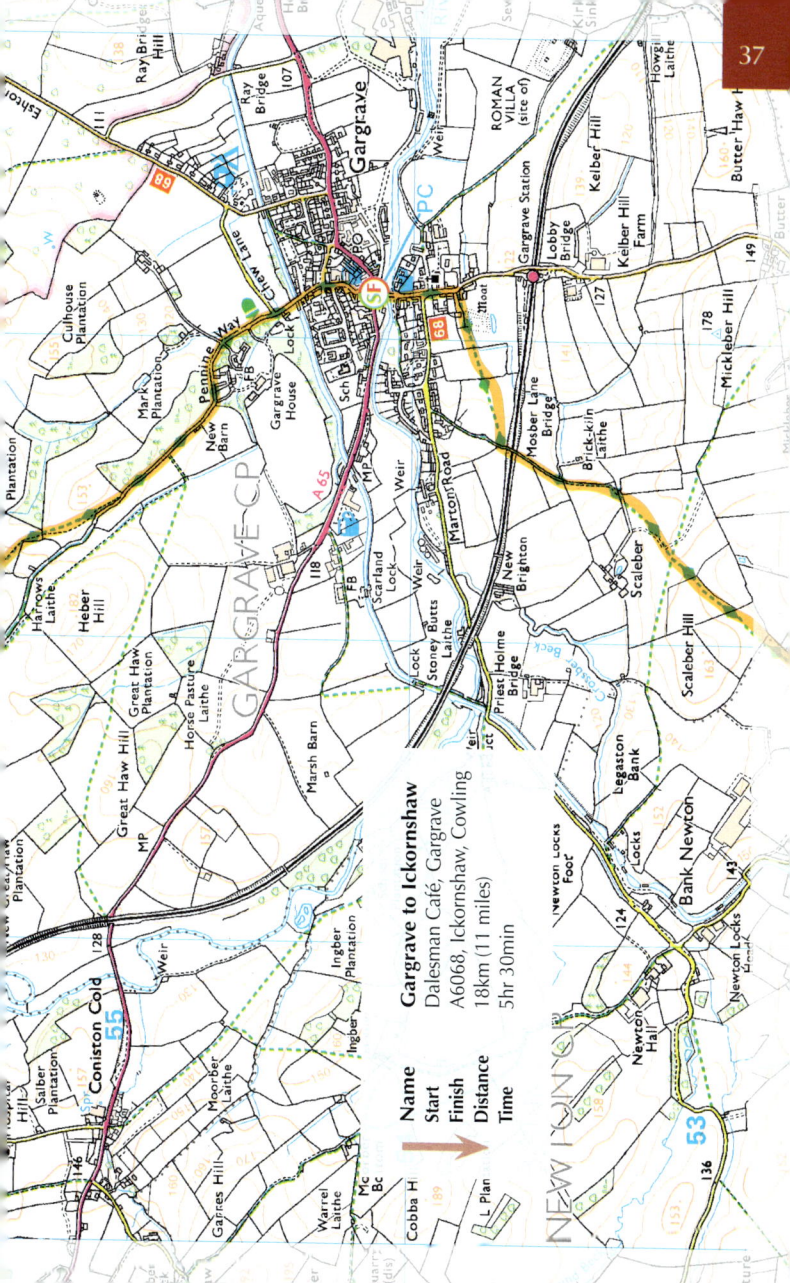

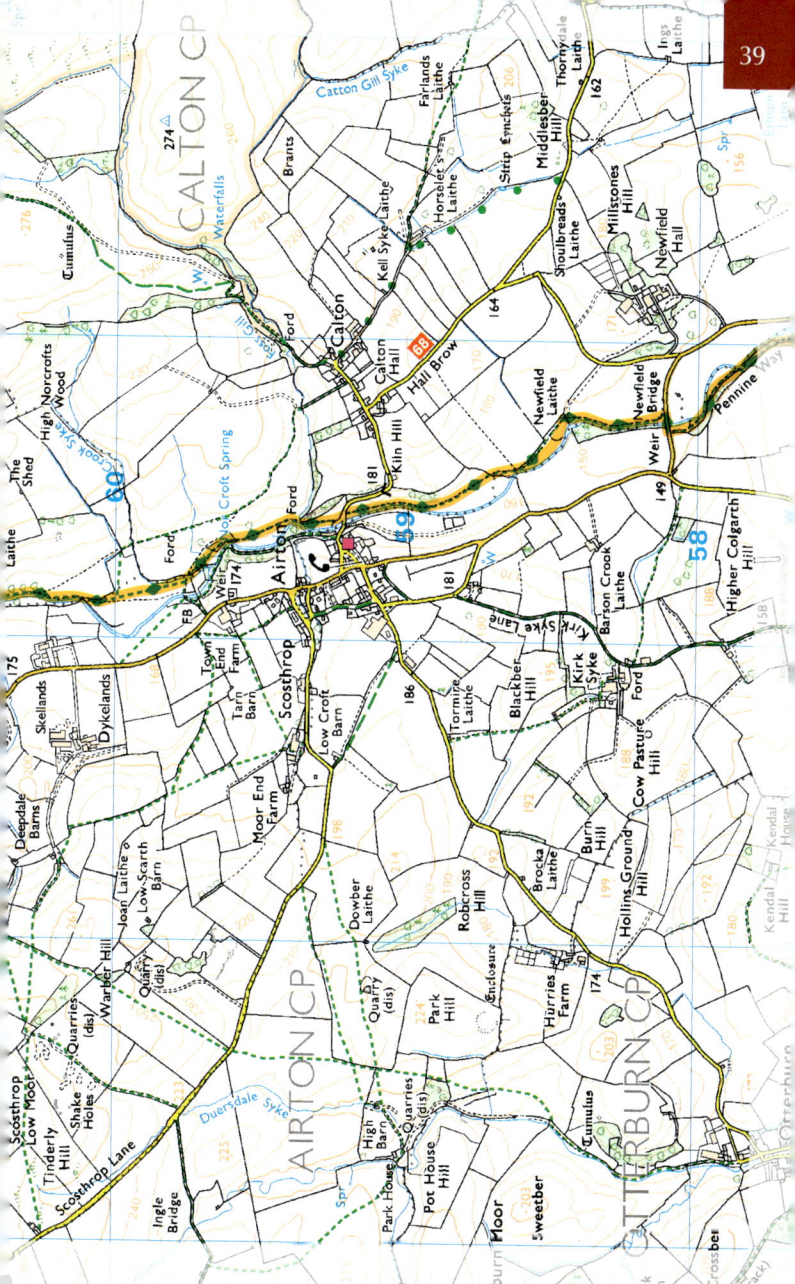

40

41

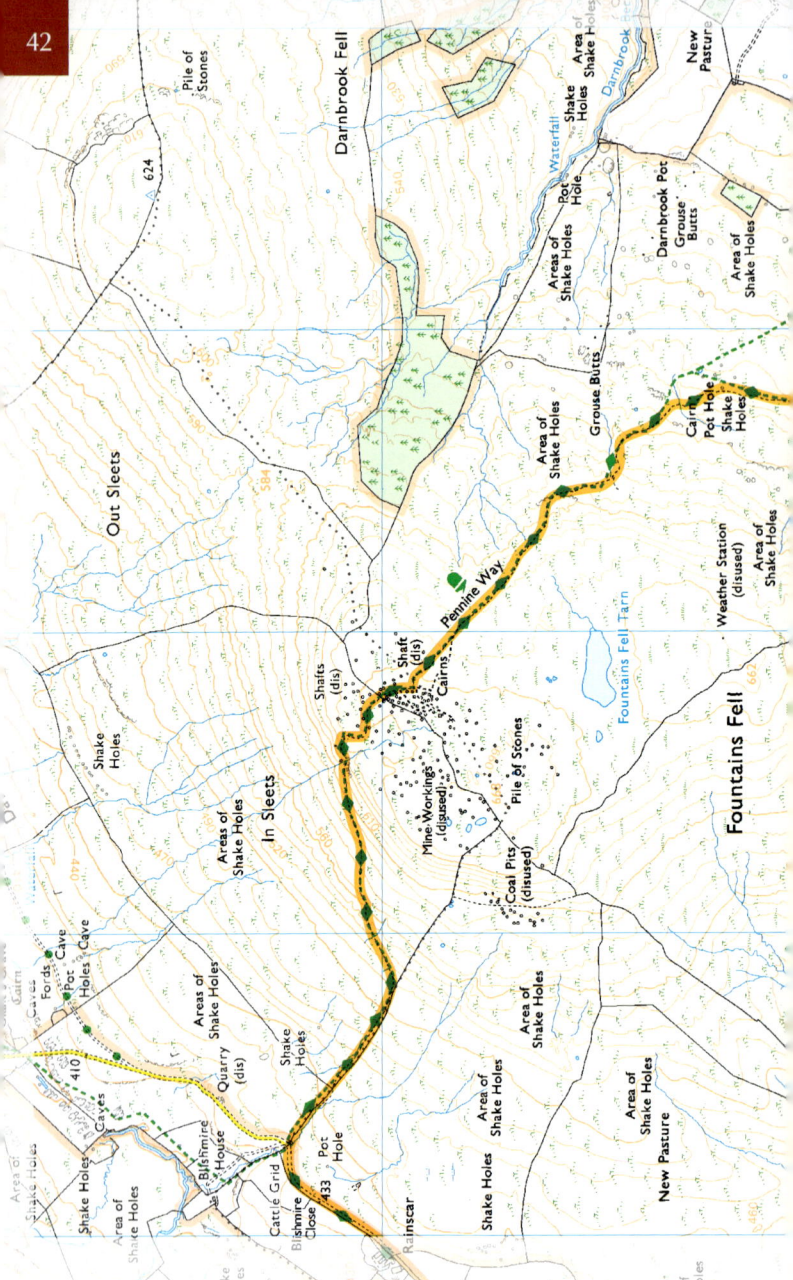

43

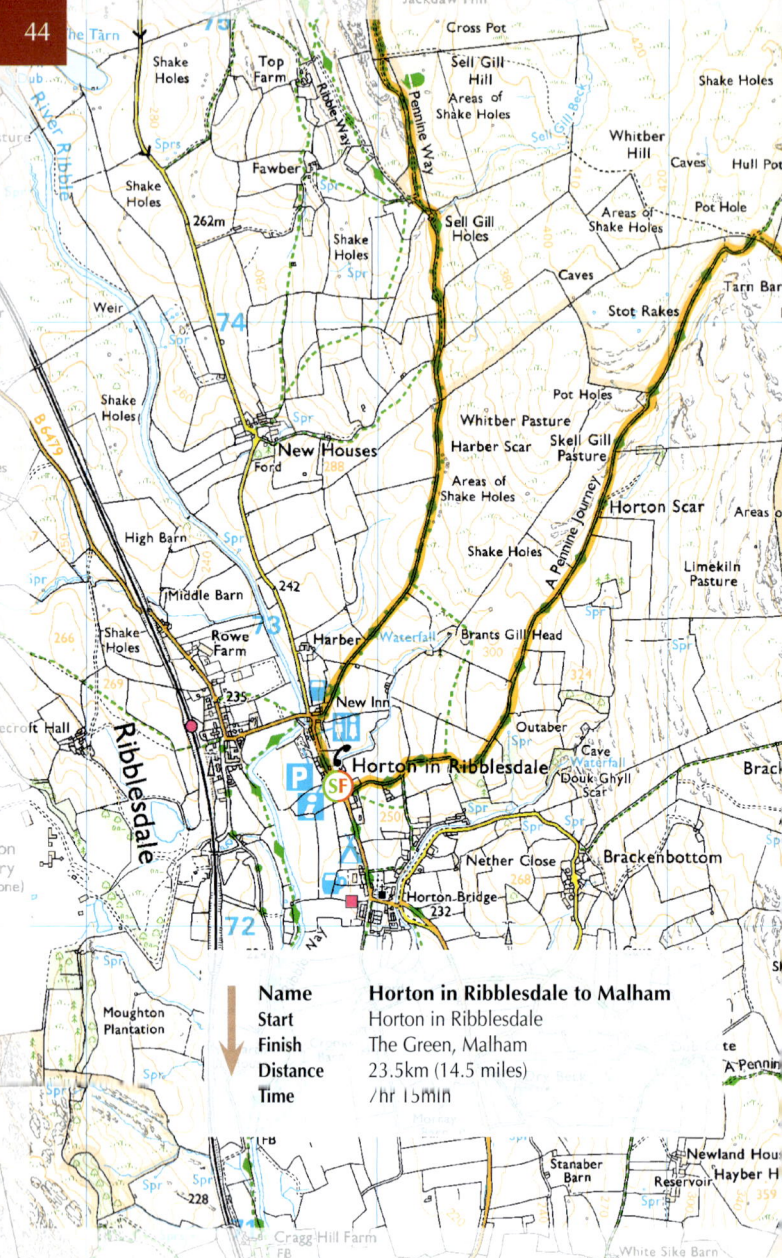

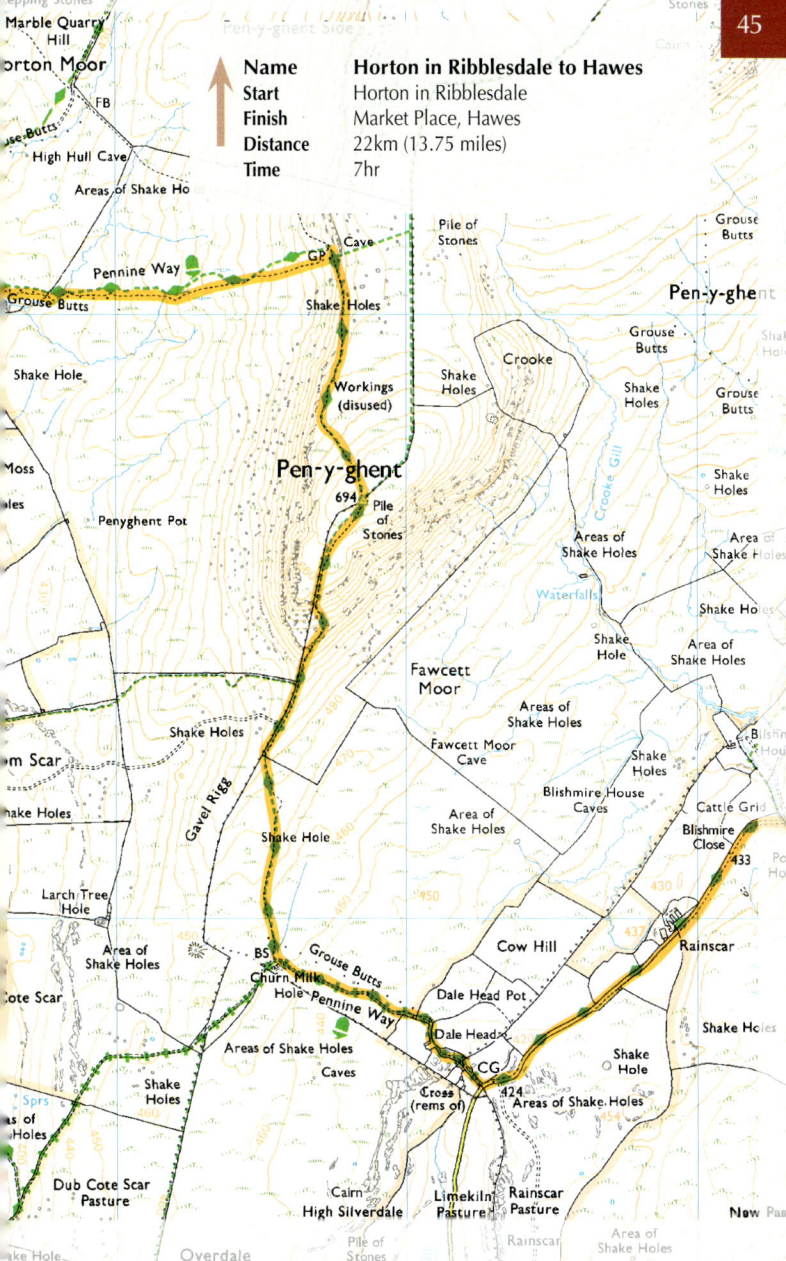

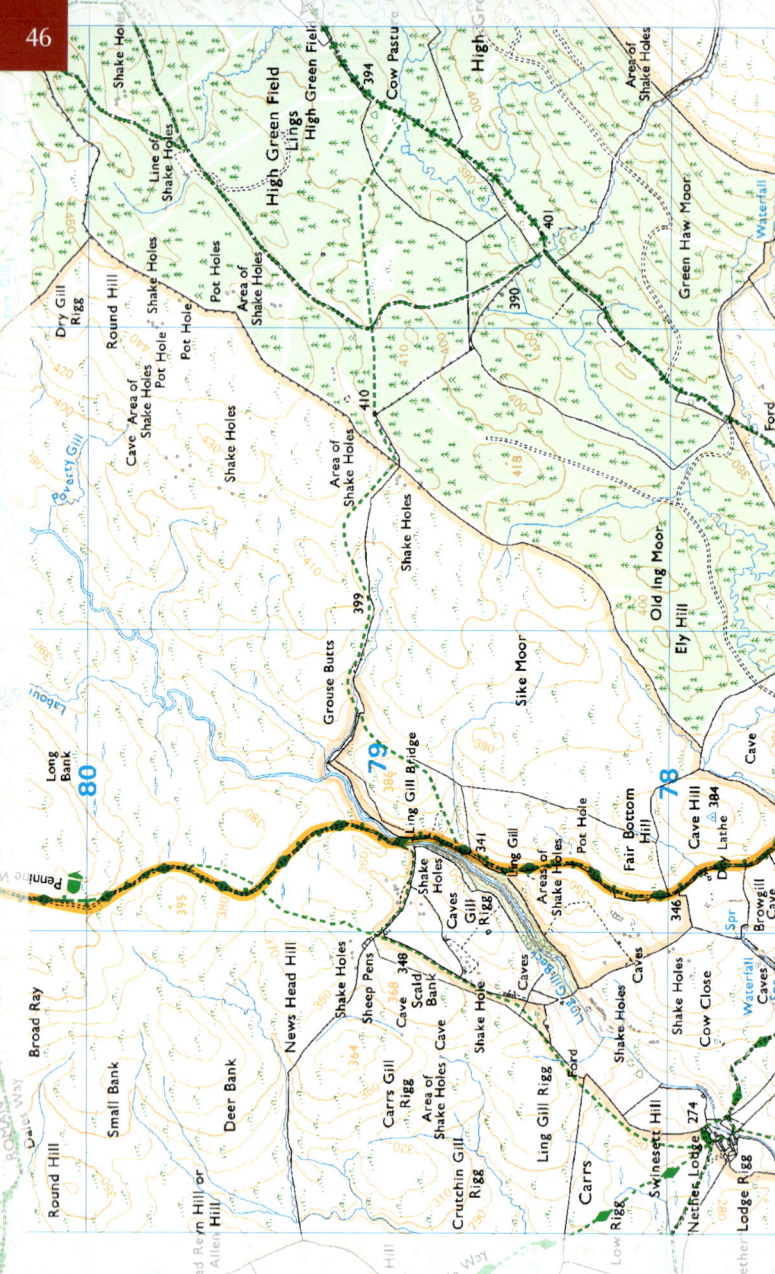

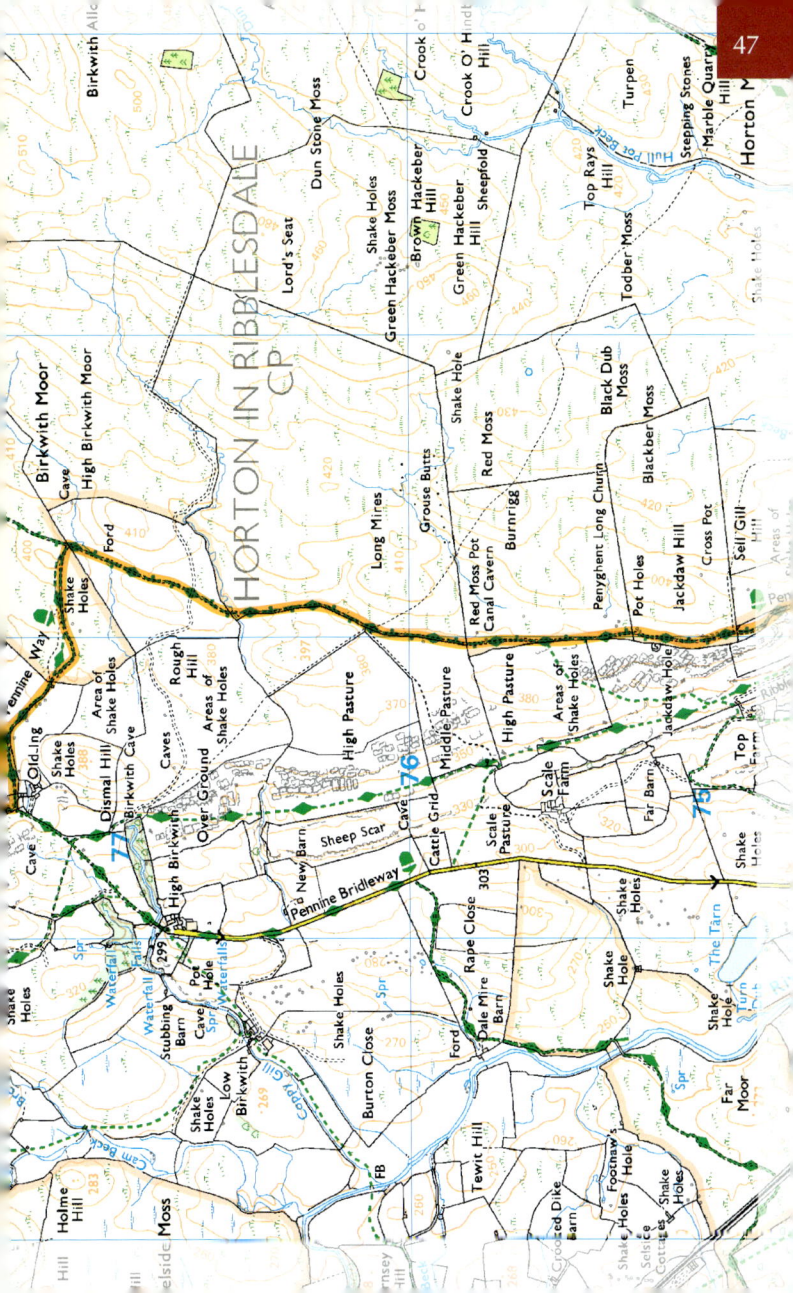

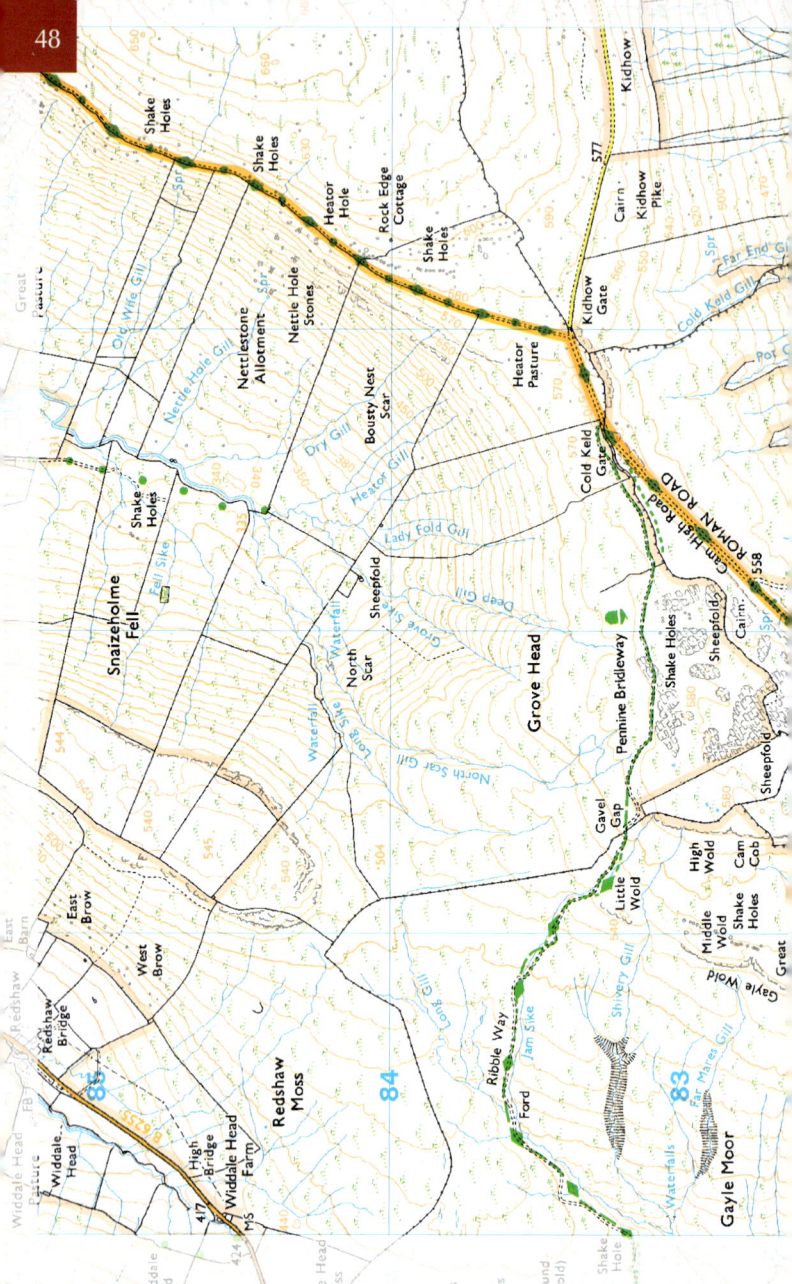

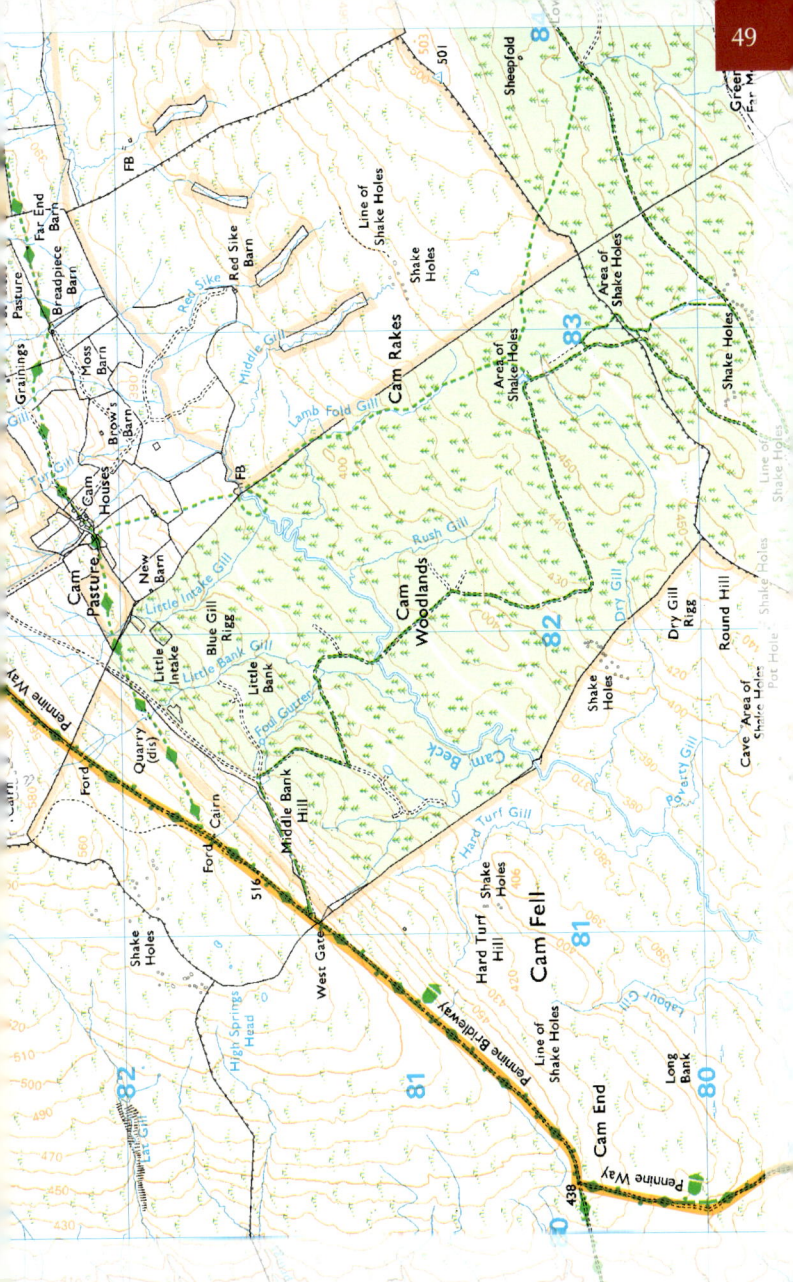

50

52

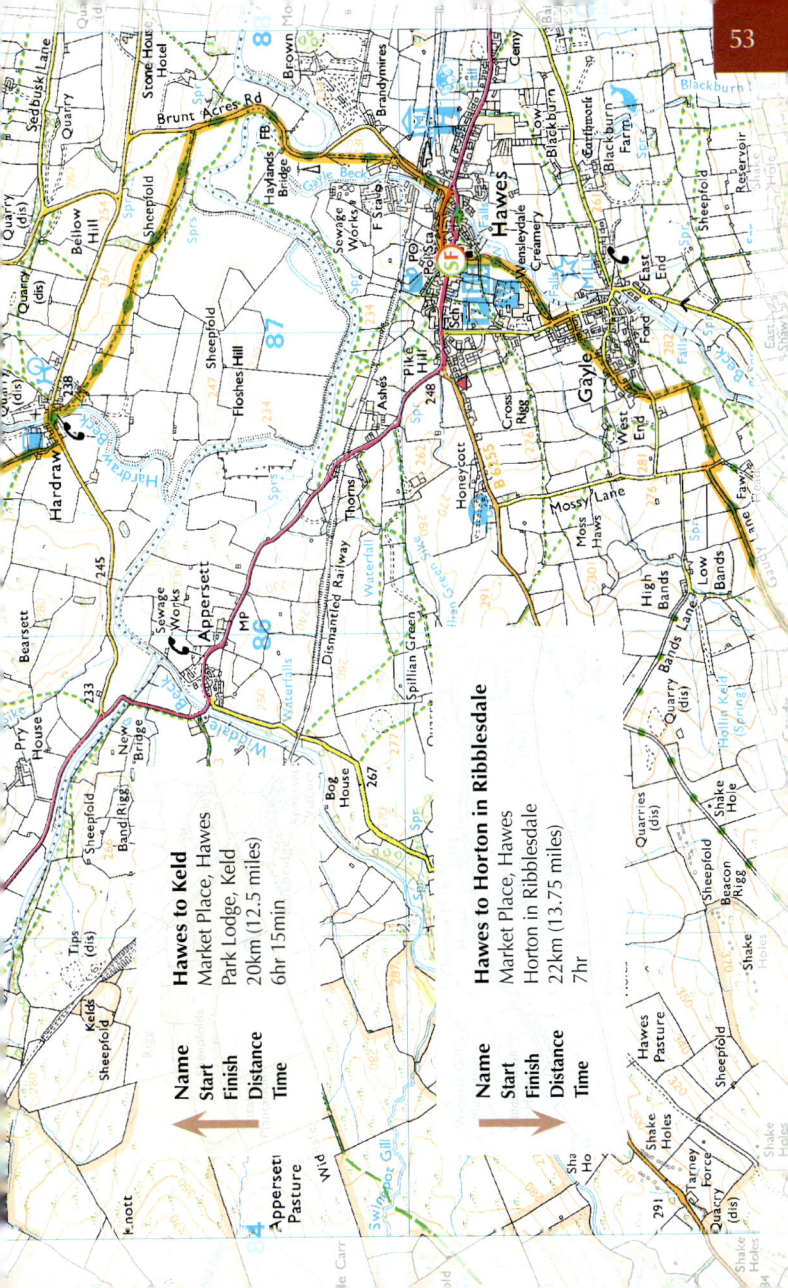

Hawes to Keld
Market Place, Hawes
Park Lodge, Keld
20km (12.5 miles)
6hr 15min

Name
Start
Finish
Distance
Time

Hawes to Horton in Ribblesdale
Market Place, Hawes
Horton in Ribblesdale
22km (13.75 miles)
7hr

Name
Start
Finish
Distance
Time

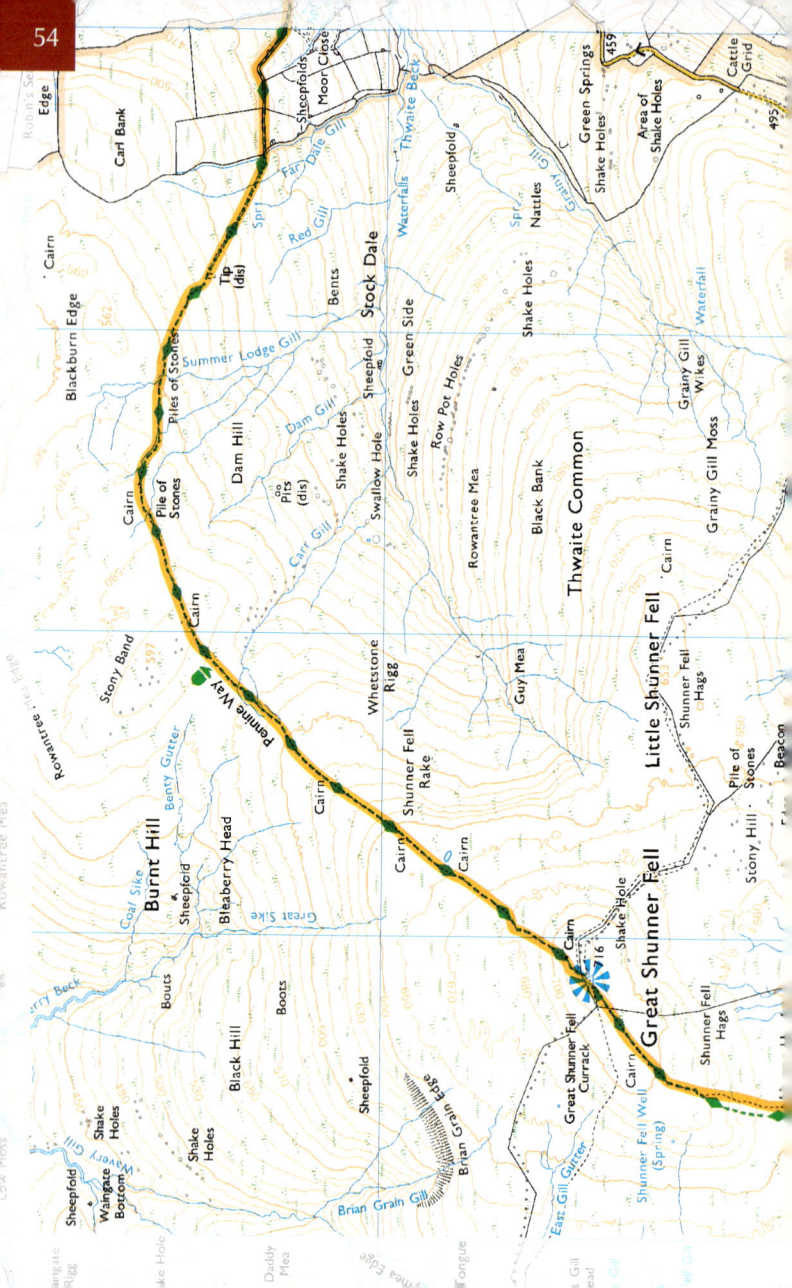

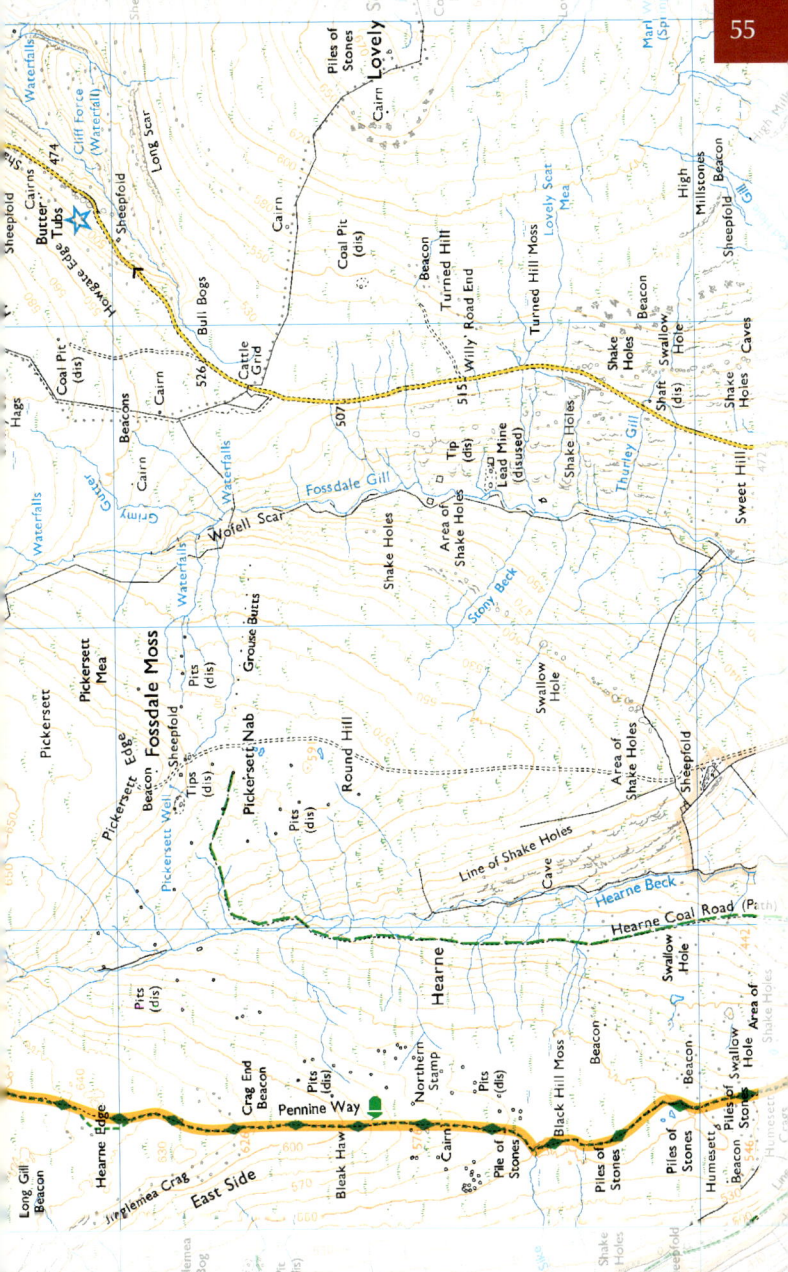

Name
Start Park Lodge, Keld
Finish Lay-by, Clove Lodge, Baldersdale or St Giles' Church, Bowes

Distance 23km (14.25 miles) or 20.5km (12¾ miles)
Time 7hr or 6hr 30min

Keld to Baldersdale or Bowes

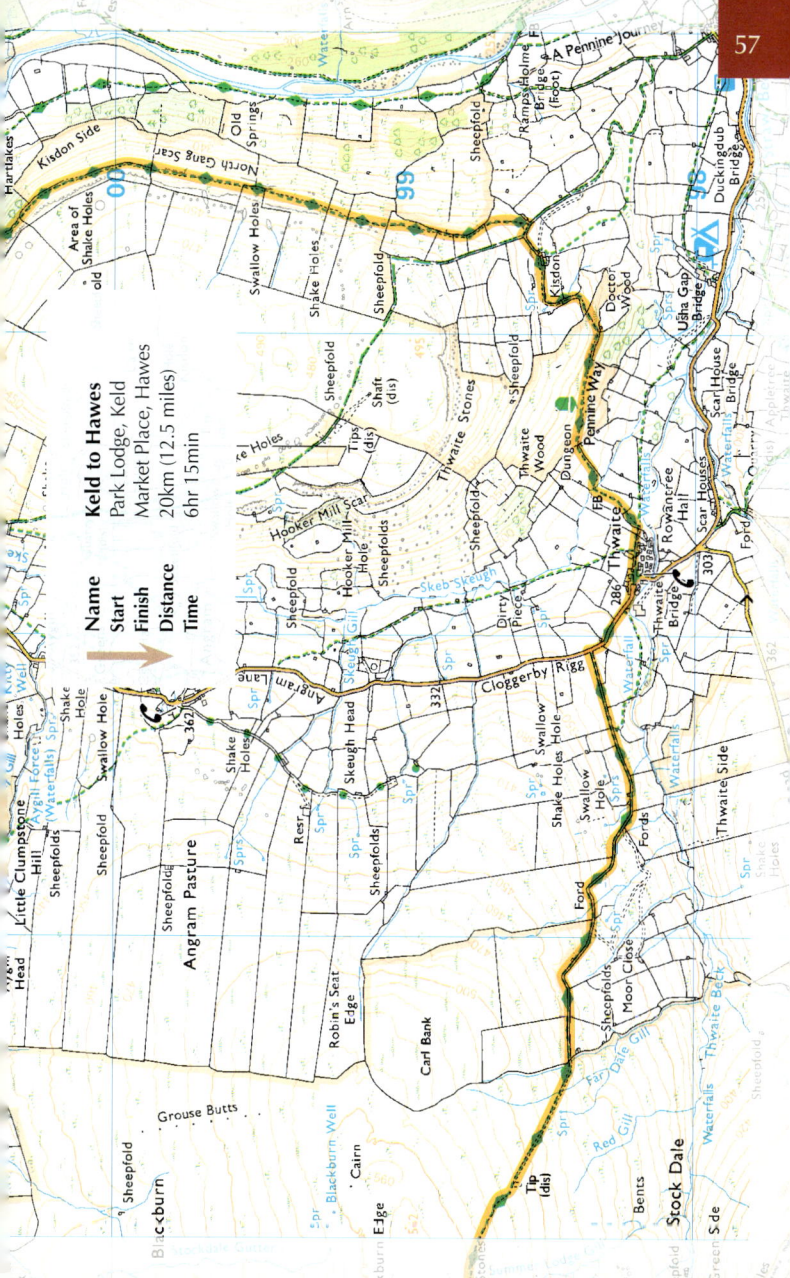

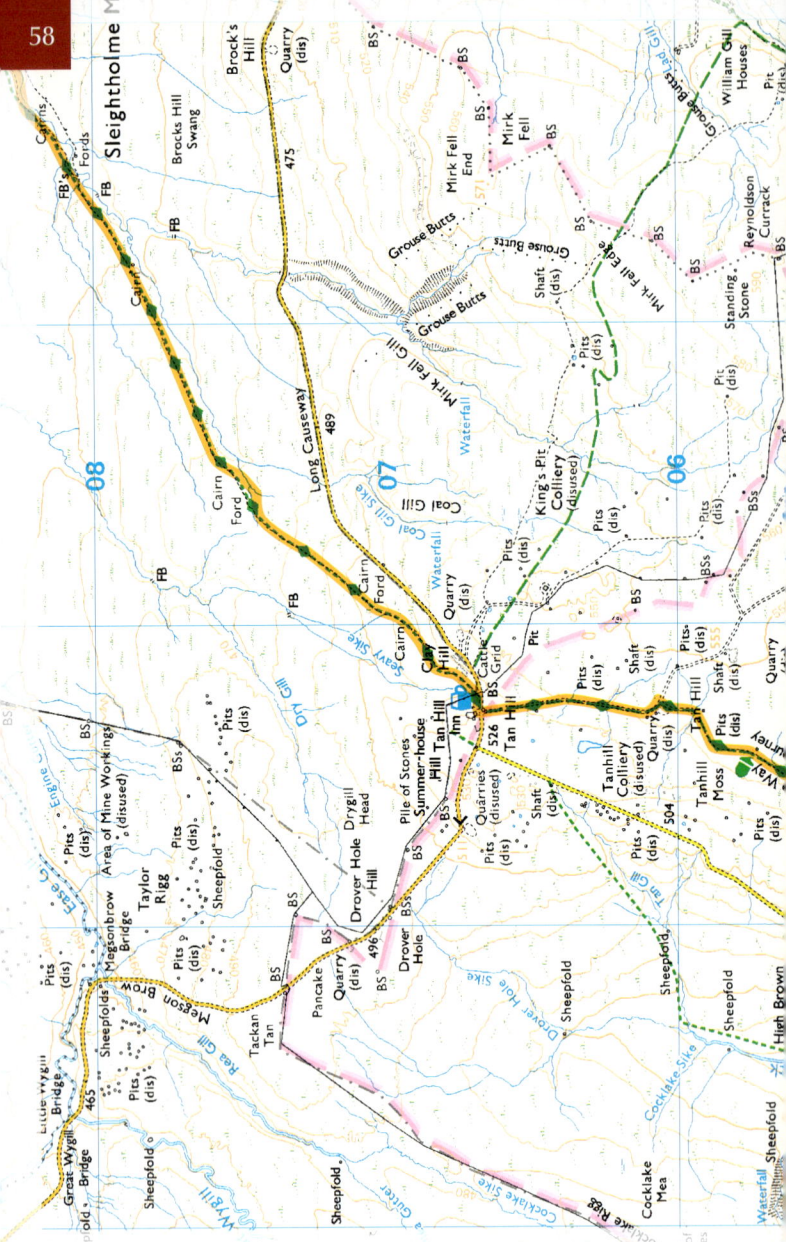

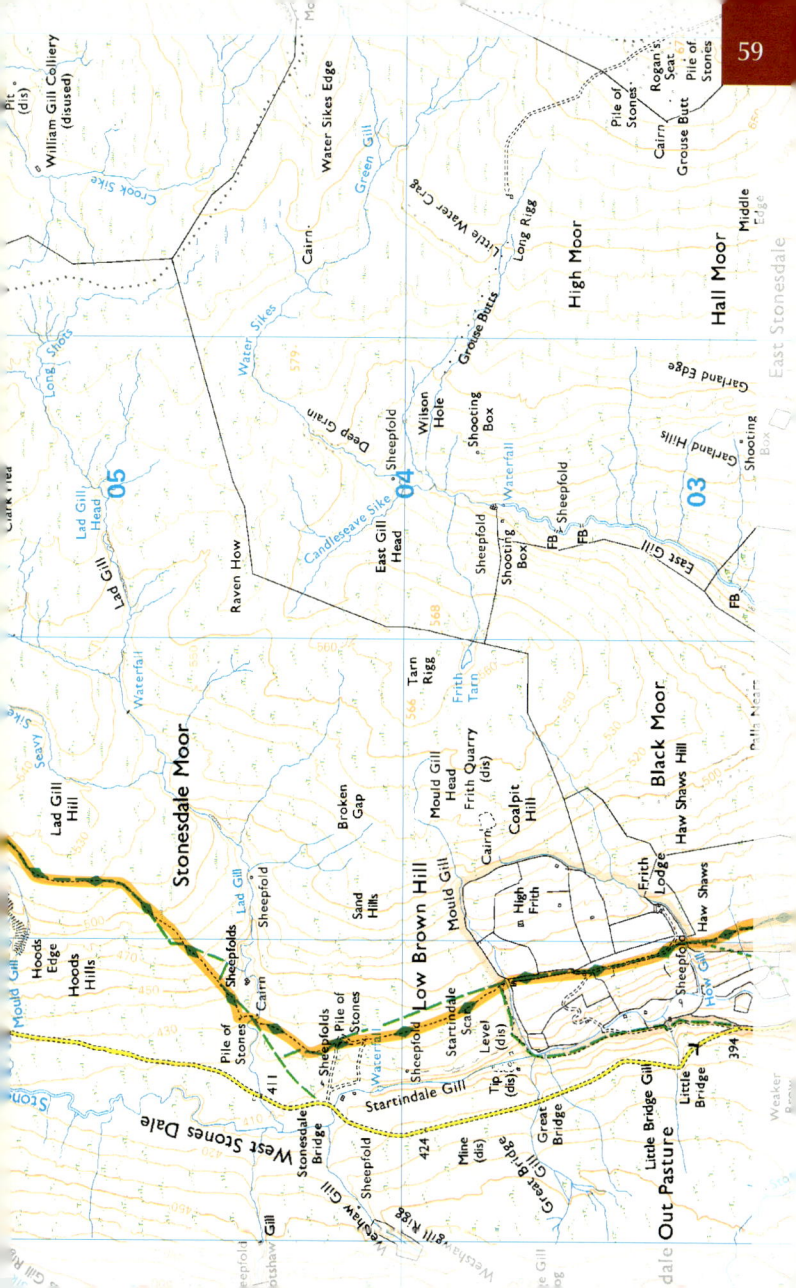

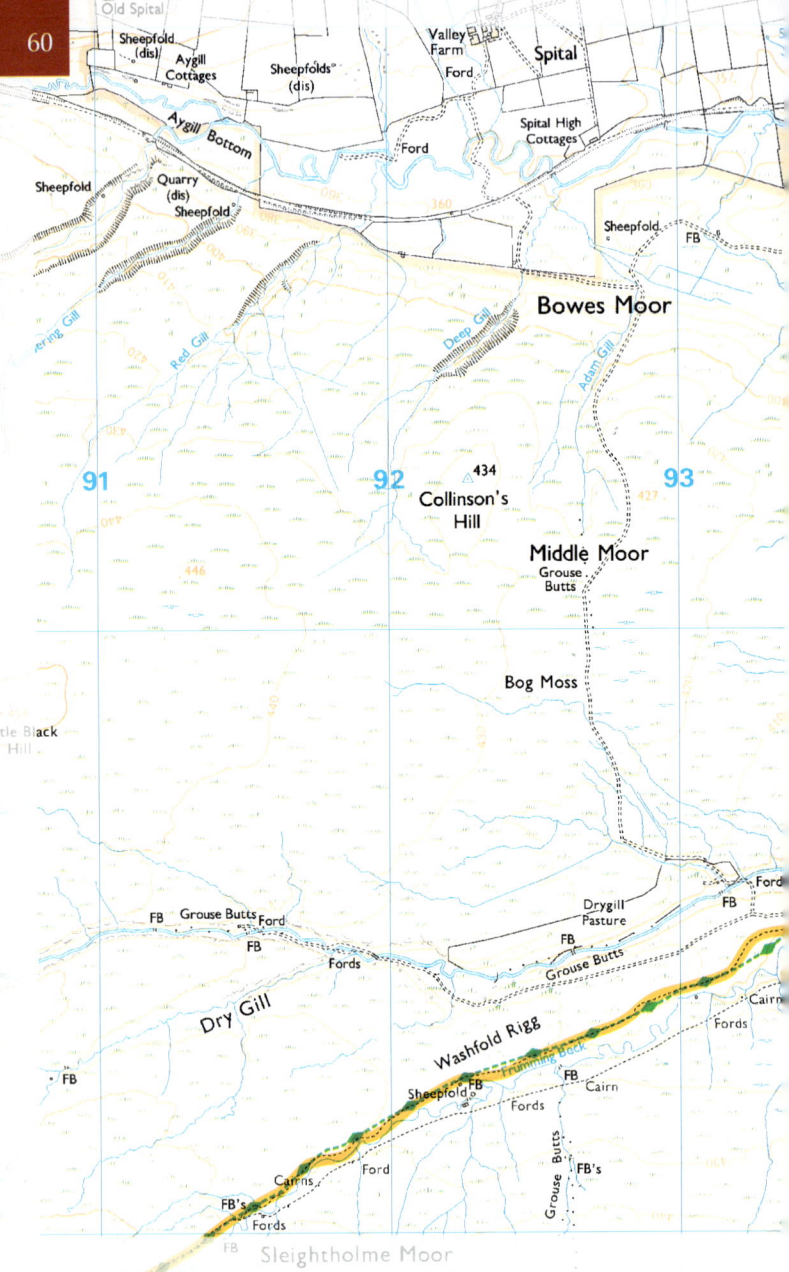

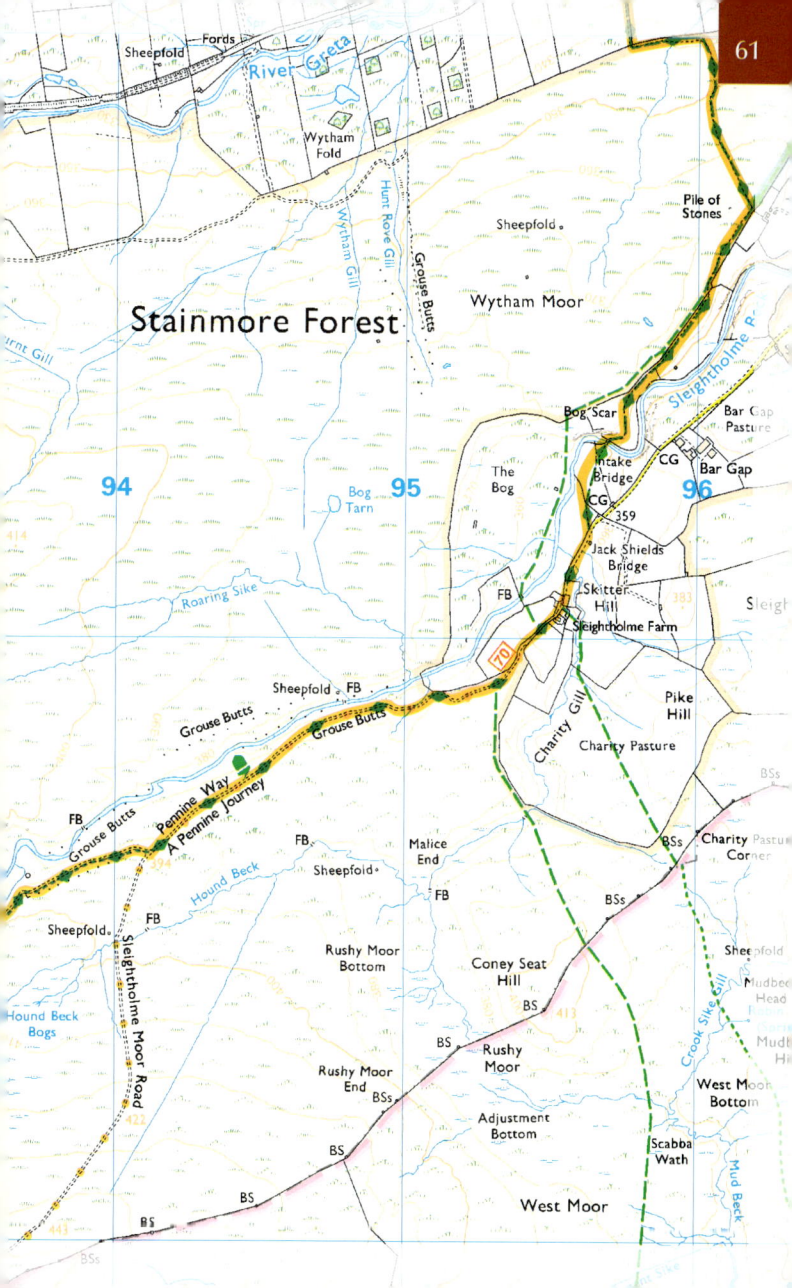

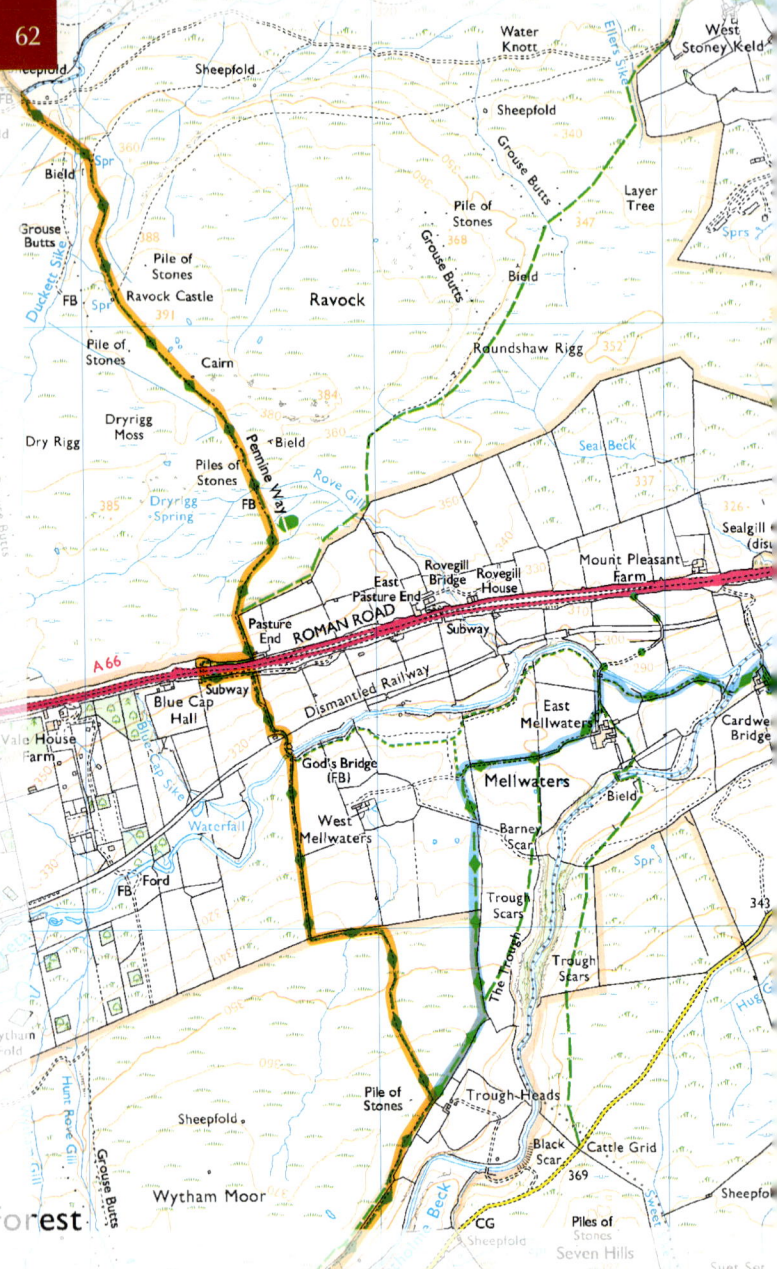

↑	**Name**	**Bowes to Middleton-in-Teesdale**
	Start	St Giles' Church, Bowes
	Finish	Horsemarket, Middleton-in-Teesdale
	Distance	19.5km (12 miles))
	Time	6hr

↓	**Name**	**Bowes to Keld**
	Start	St Giles' Church, Bowes
	Finish	Park Lodge, Keld
	Distance	20.5km (12.75 miles)
	Time	6hr 30min

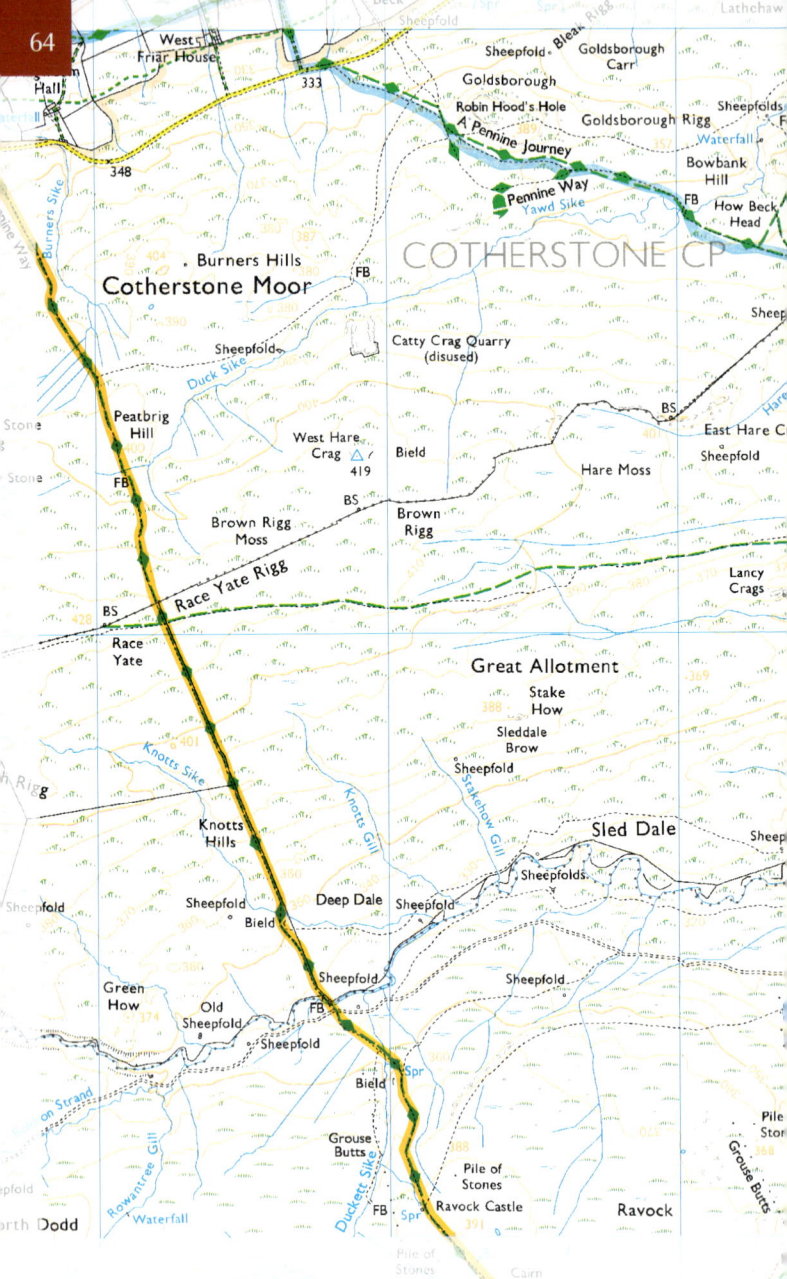

65

- Loups's Crag
- Tinklers Quarry (disused)
- Loups's Hill
- Sunny Brow
- Ford
- East Loups's
- FB
- Butts
- Scur Beck
- Grouse Butts
- Ravock Plantation
- Sheepfold
- Moby Well (Spring)
- Long Rigg
- West Loups's
- Sprs
- Ford
- Ravock Rigg
- DANGER AREA
- FB
- Gill Feet
- Gill Beck
- Whitstone Rigg
- Kearton Rigg
- Loup's Plantation
- Stonefold Rigg
- Battle Hill
- old Rigg
- Stable Sike
- Kirkstreveland Rigg
- Spr
- Scotty Rigg
- adyfold Crags
- Hazelgill Beck
- LARTINGTON CP
- Nova Scotia
- Hazelgill Rigg
- Windbreak
- Hazelgill
- Spr
- Deepdale Beck
- Ford
- FB
- Levy Pool
- Sheepfold
- Strand Foot
- Stoney Keld
- Spr
- Spr
- Crag Bridge
- Fount Hea
- Stonykeld Spring
- West Stoney Keld
- Tute Hill
- East Stoney Keld
- Stony Keld
- 303
- Ellers Sike
- Storage Site (disused)
- Layer Tree
- Philip Hill
- Sprs
- Clint House
- Clint Lane
- 70
- Brookside
- Stone
- The Old Moss
- Stone
- Quarry

66

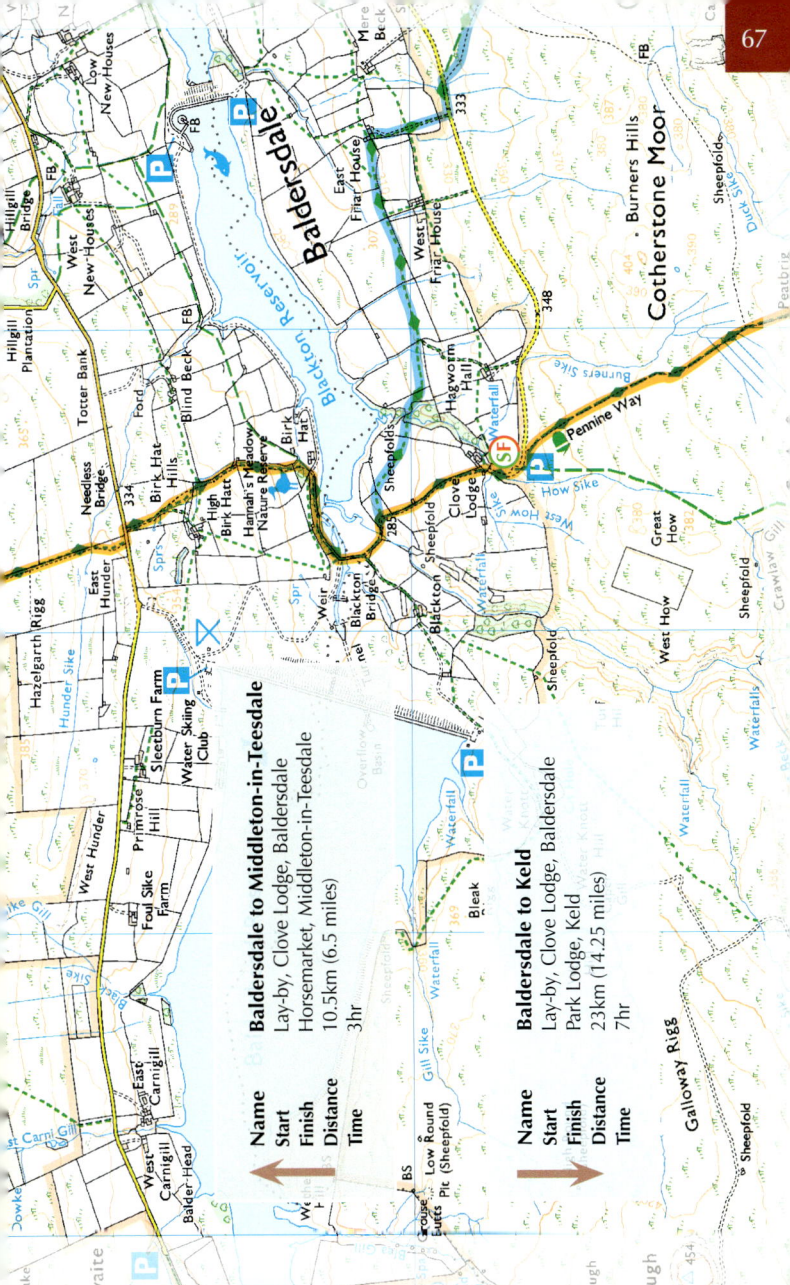

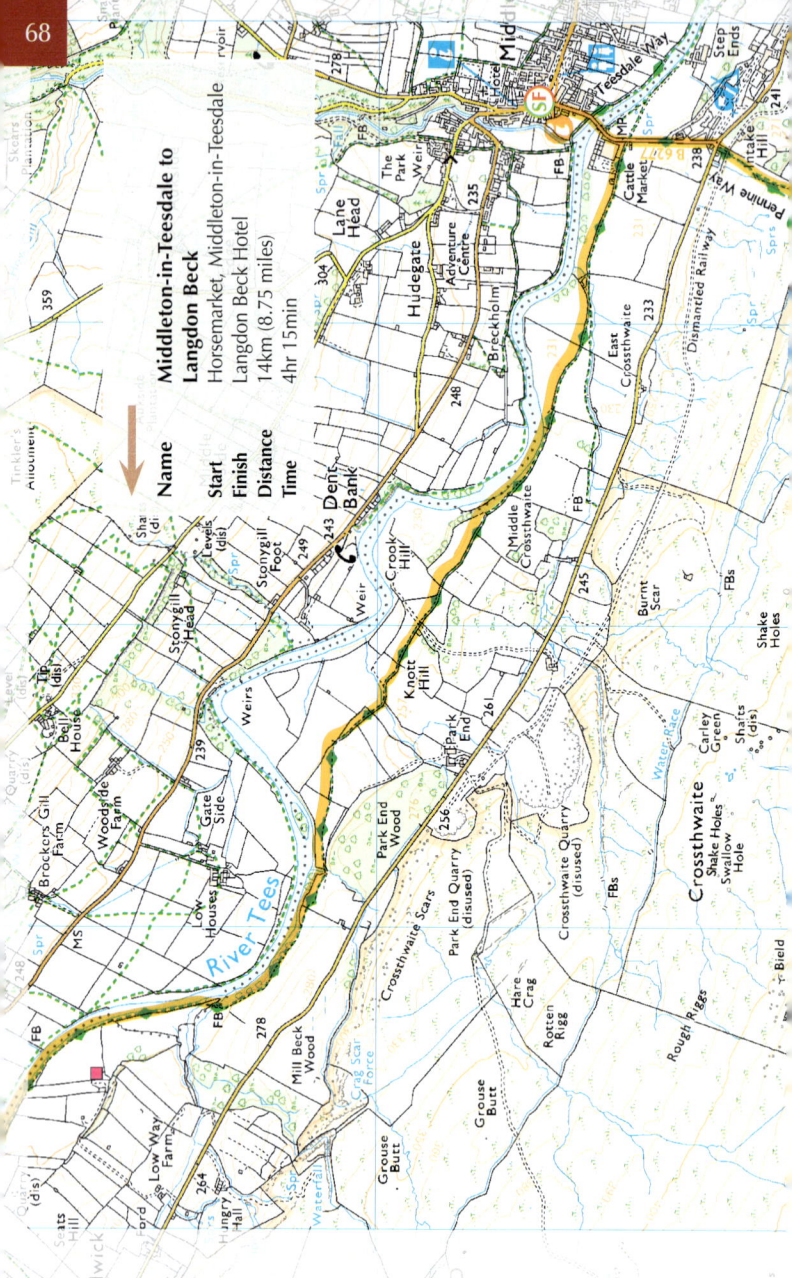

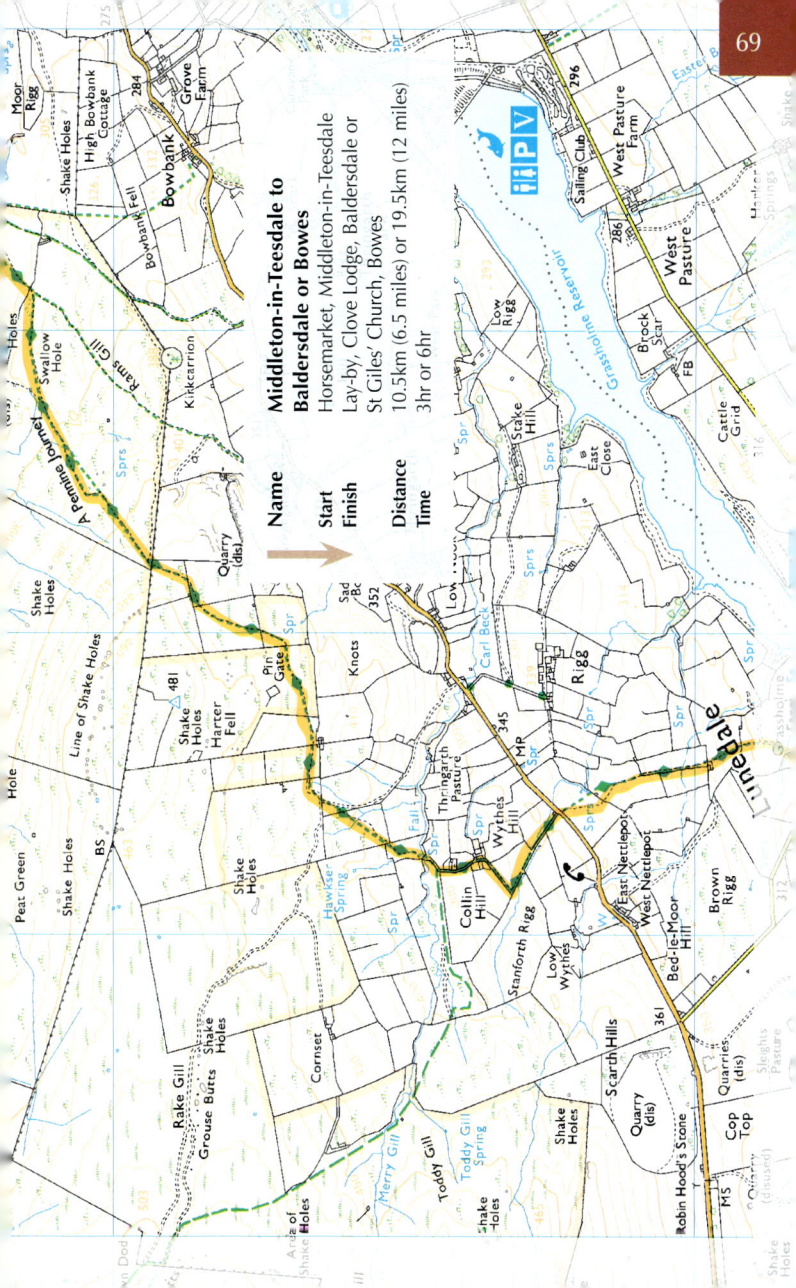

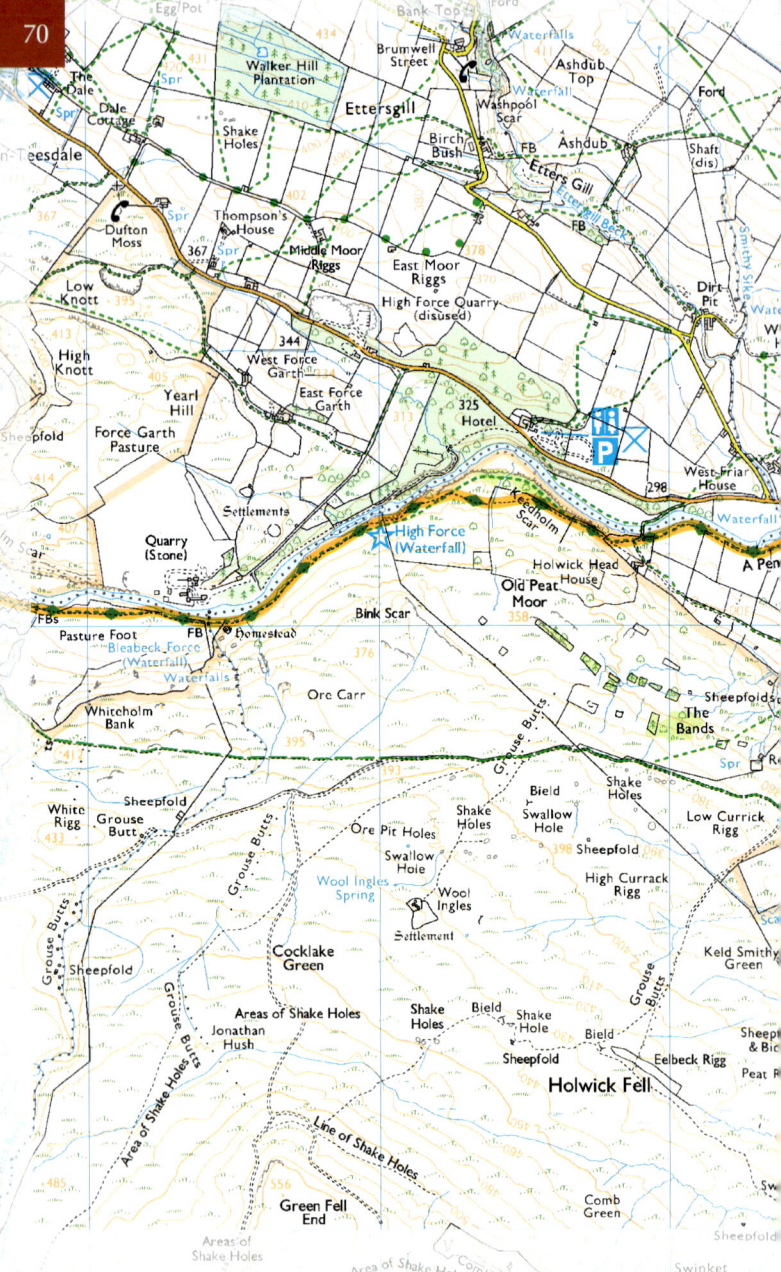

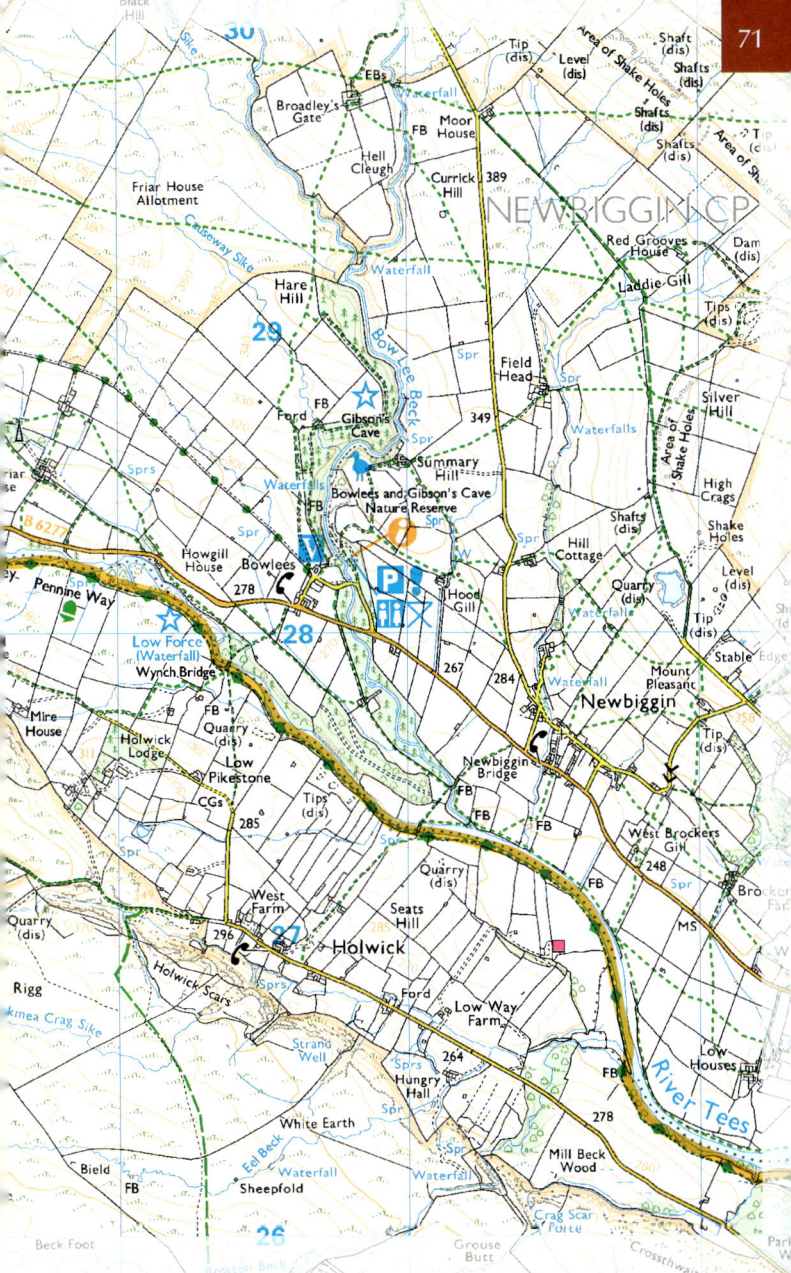

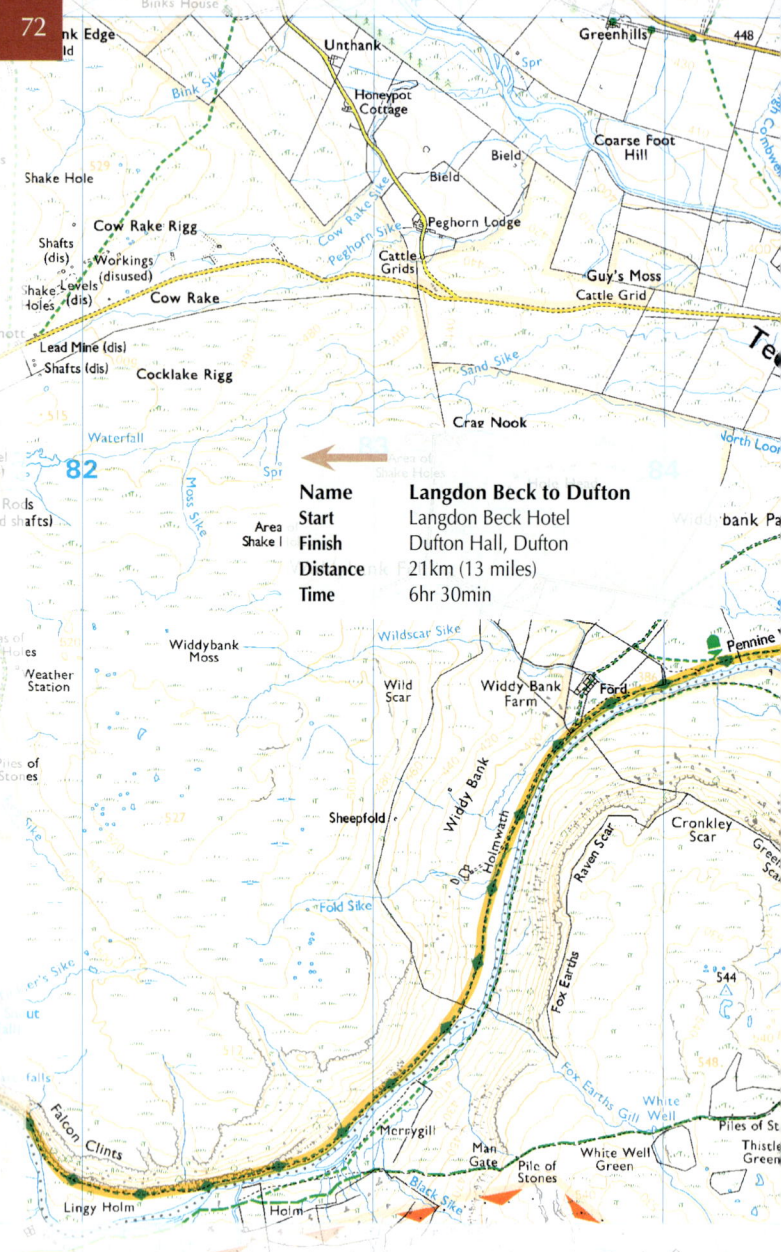

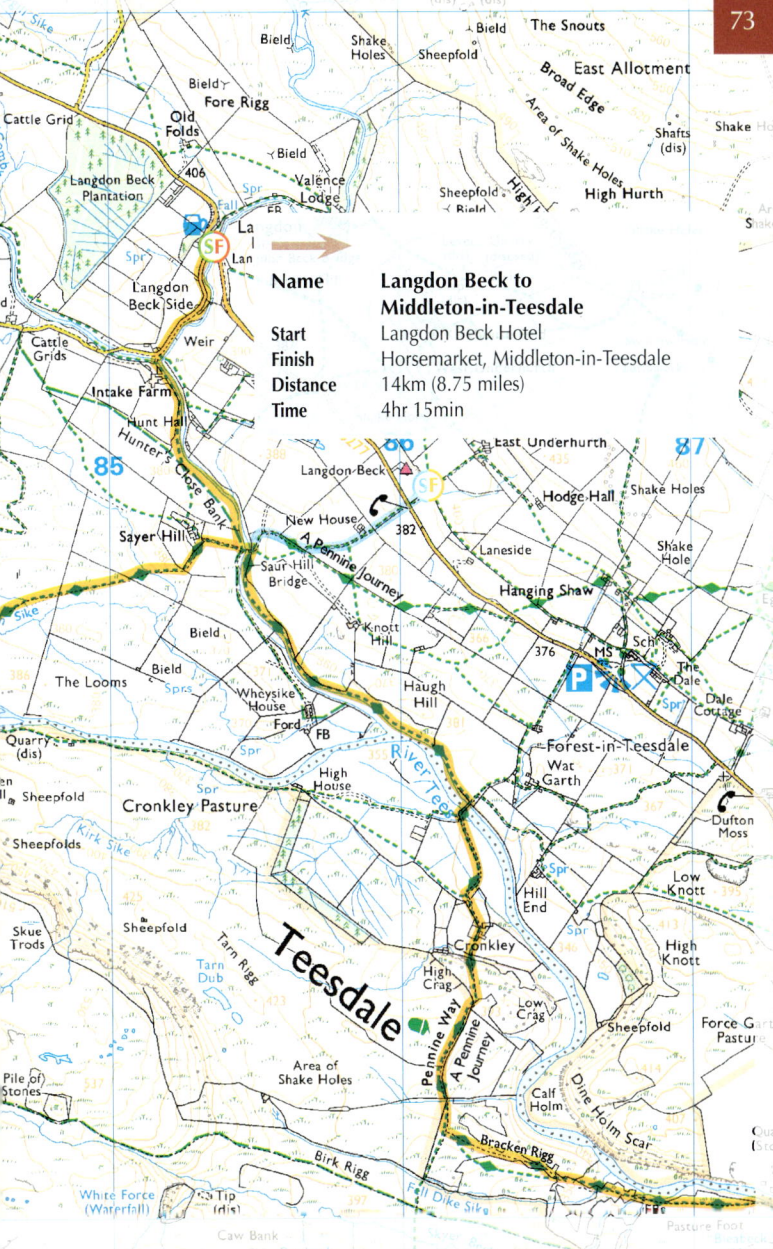

Name	**Langdon Beck to Middleton-in-Teesdale**
Start	Langdon Beck Hotel
Finish	Horsemarket, Middleton-in-Teesdale
Distance	14km (8.75 miles)
Time	4hr 15min

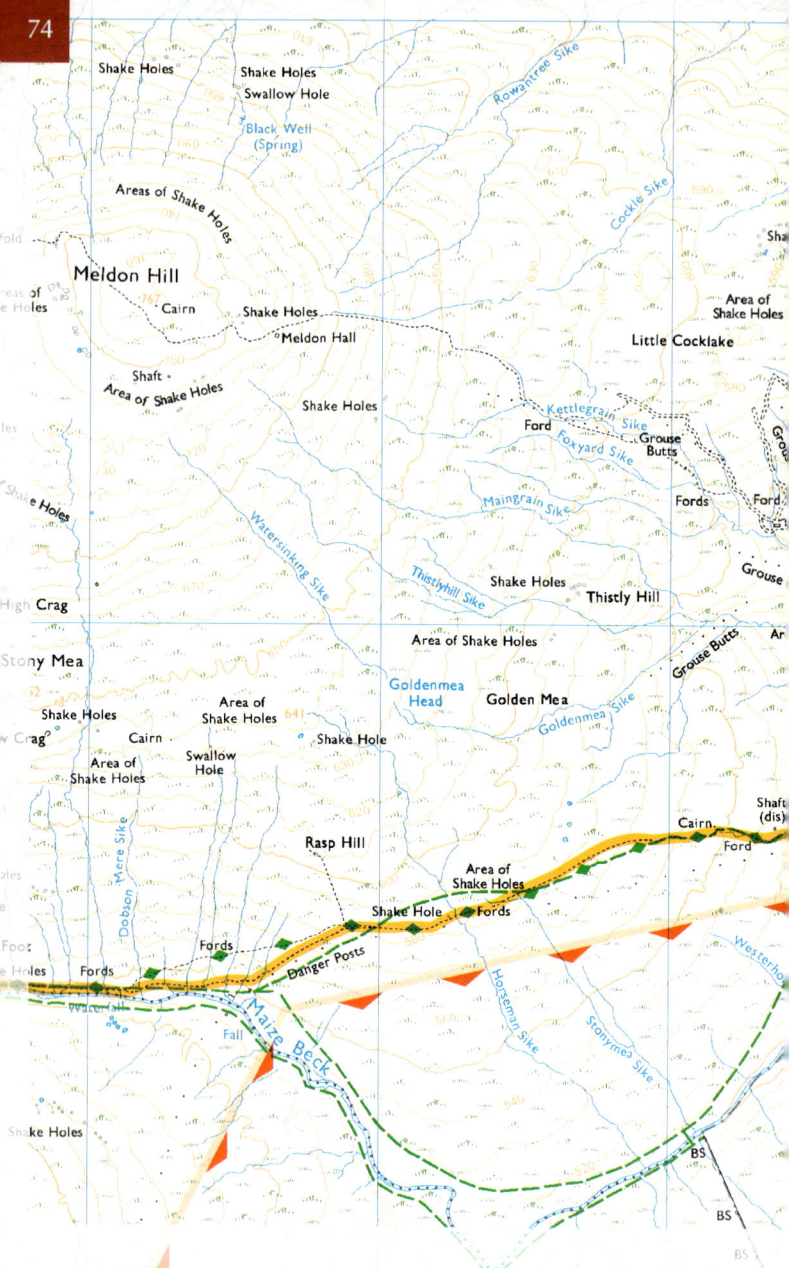

Map 75

Grid squares: 25, 27, 28, 29, 30

Labels (north to south, approximately)

- Areas of Shake Holes
- Weather Station
- Furness Lodge
- Deadcrook Sike
- Whitespot Sike
- Far Foolmire
- Whitespot Fold
- Piles of Stones
- Red Sike
- Great Cocklake
- Area of Shake Holes
- Long Mea
- Near Foolmire
- East Shelvingmea
- Areas of Shake Holes
- Shake Hole
- Shake Hole
- Cow Green Dam
- Weirs
- Tinkler's Sike
- Cauldron Snout (Waterfall)
- West Shelvingmea
- Shelvingmea Sike
- Cocklake Sike
- Waterfalls
- Falcon Clints
- Waterfall
- Sheepfold
- Sheepfold
- **Pennine Way**
- Dale Byre
- Maize Beck
- Black Hill
- Lingy Holm
- Ford
- Shake Holes
- Shafts (dis)
- Hush
- Birkdale
- Waterfall
- FB
- Waterfall
- Grain Beck
- Danger Posts
- Shafts (dis)
- Birkdale Hush
- Moss Sike
- Waterfalls
- Maizebeck Force
- Line of Shake Holes
- Sheepfold
- Merrygill Moss
- Area of Shake Holes
- Crook Sike
- Dam (dis)
- Pile of Stones
- Moss Shop (ruined mine)
- Waterfall
- Maizebeck Shop (ruined mine)
- Line of Shake Holes
- Area of Shake Holes
- Areas of Shake Holes
- Waterfall
- Greengill Hush
- Spr
- Cairn
- Green Lead Mines
- Greenmines Shop
- Area of Shake Holes
- Area of Shake Holes
- Shaft (dis)
- Broad Mease
- Shaft (dis)
- Shaft (dis)
- Shake Holes
- Shake Hole
- Area of Shake Holes
- Spr
- Fords
- Swallow

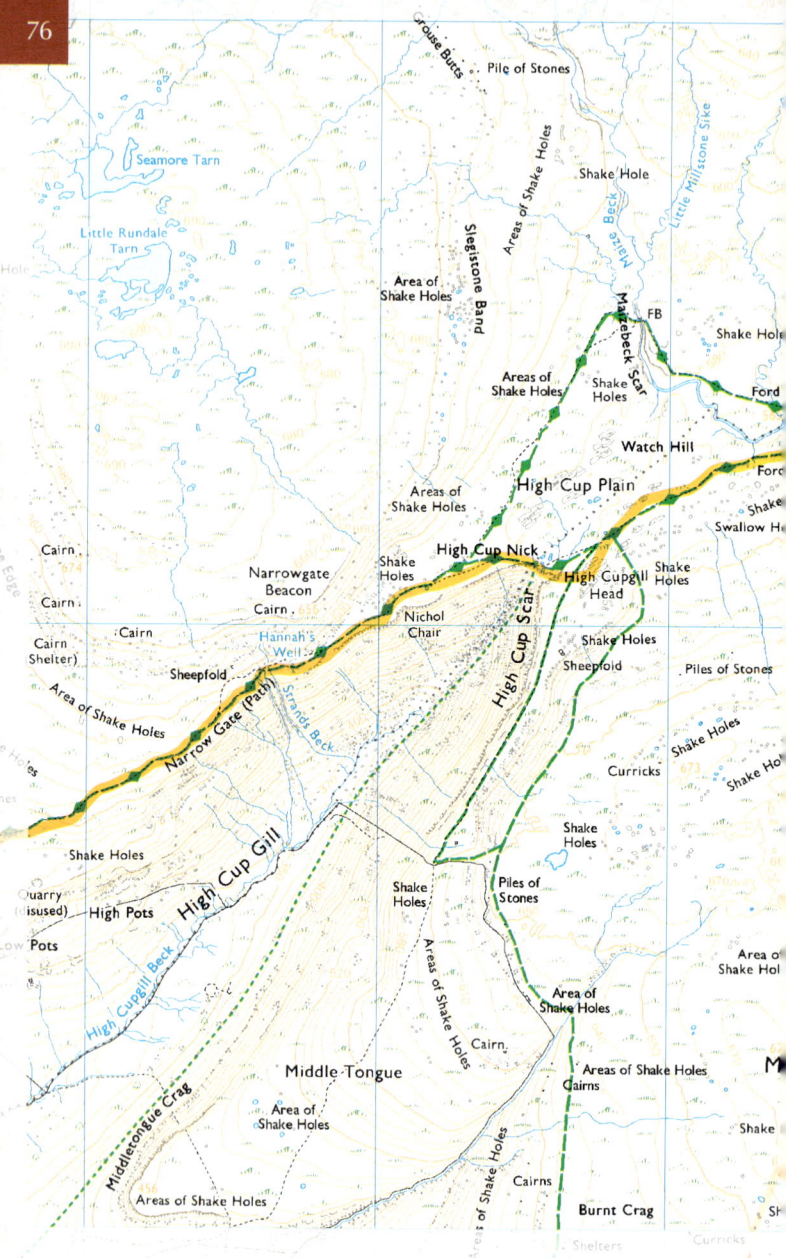

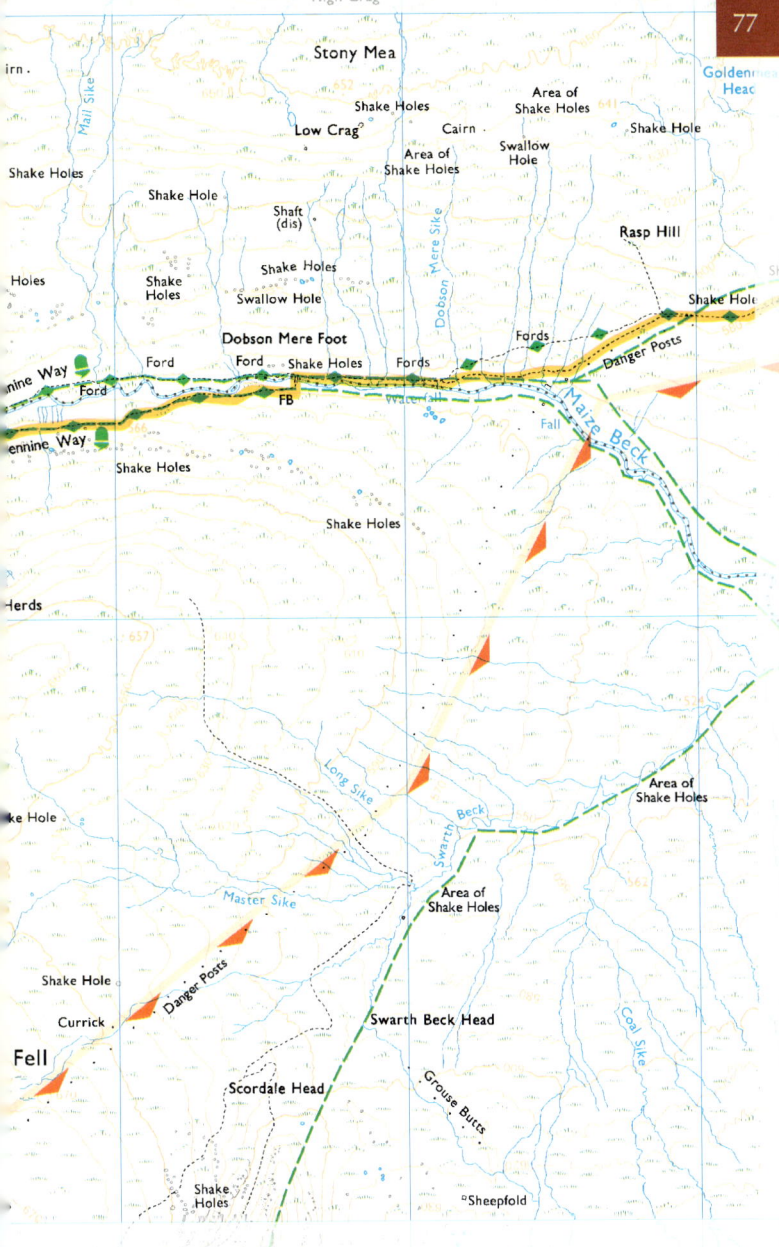

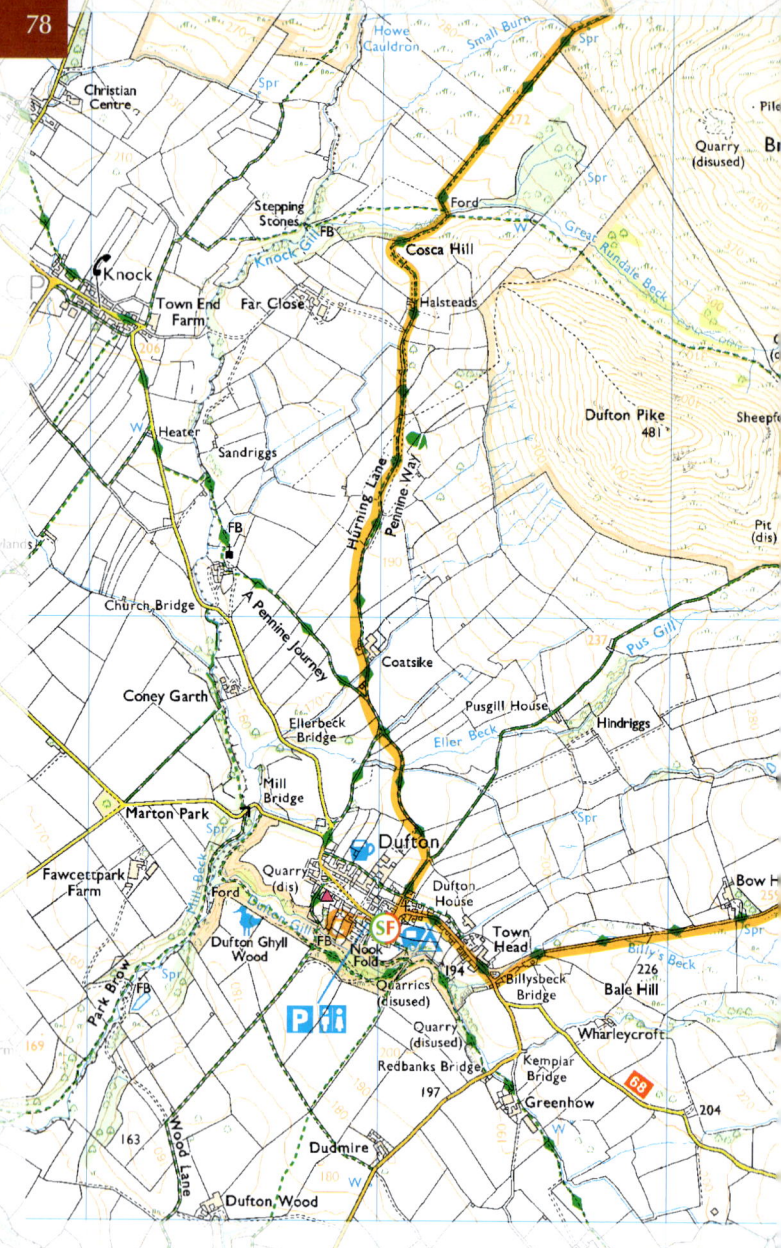

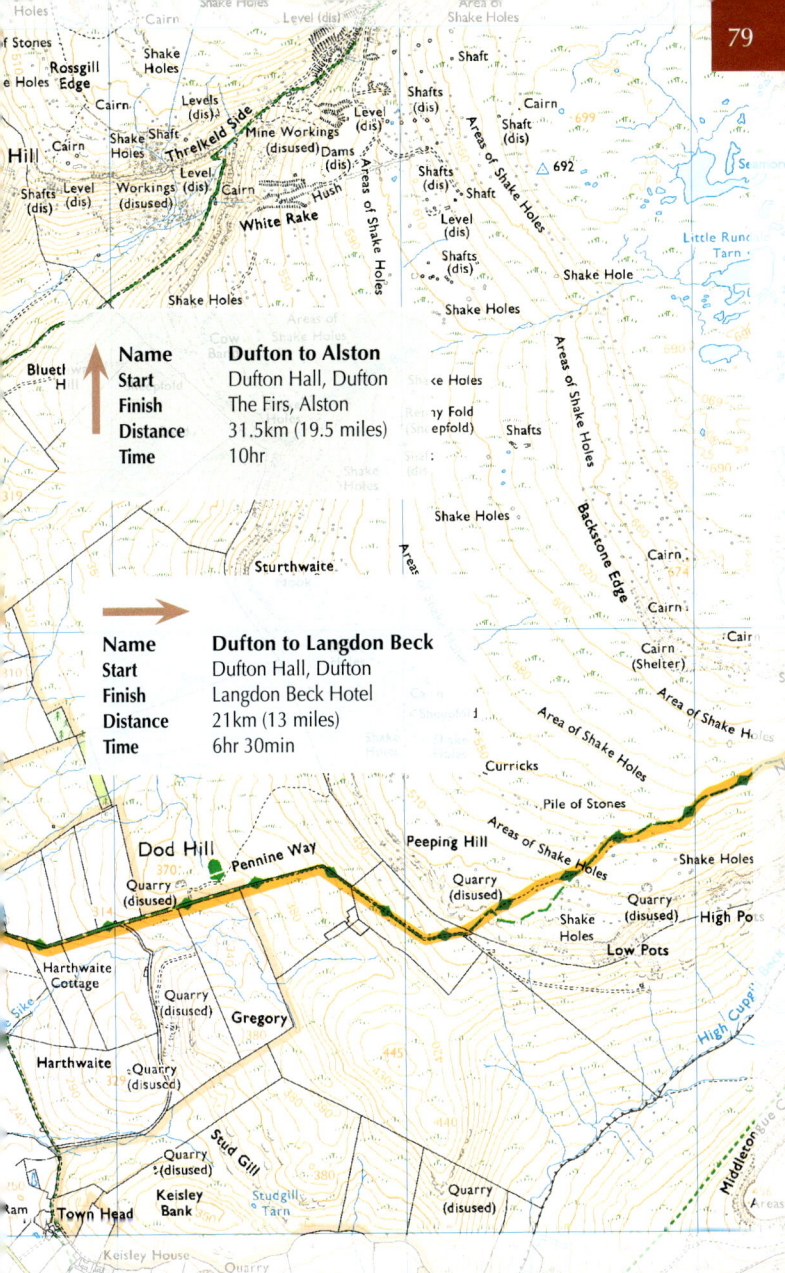

Name	**Dufton to Alston**
Start	Dufton Hall, Dufton
Finish	The Firs, Alston
Distance	31.5km (19.5 miles)
Time	10hr

Name	**Dufton to Langdon Beck**
Start	Dufton Hall, Dufton
Finish	Langdon Beck Hotel
Distance	21km (13 miles)
Time	6hr 30min

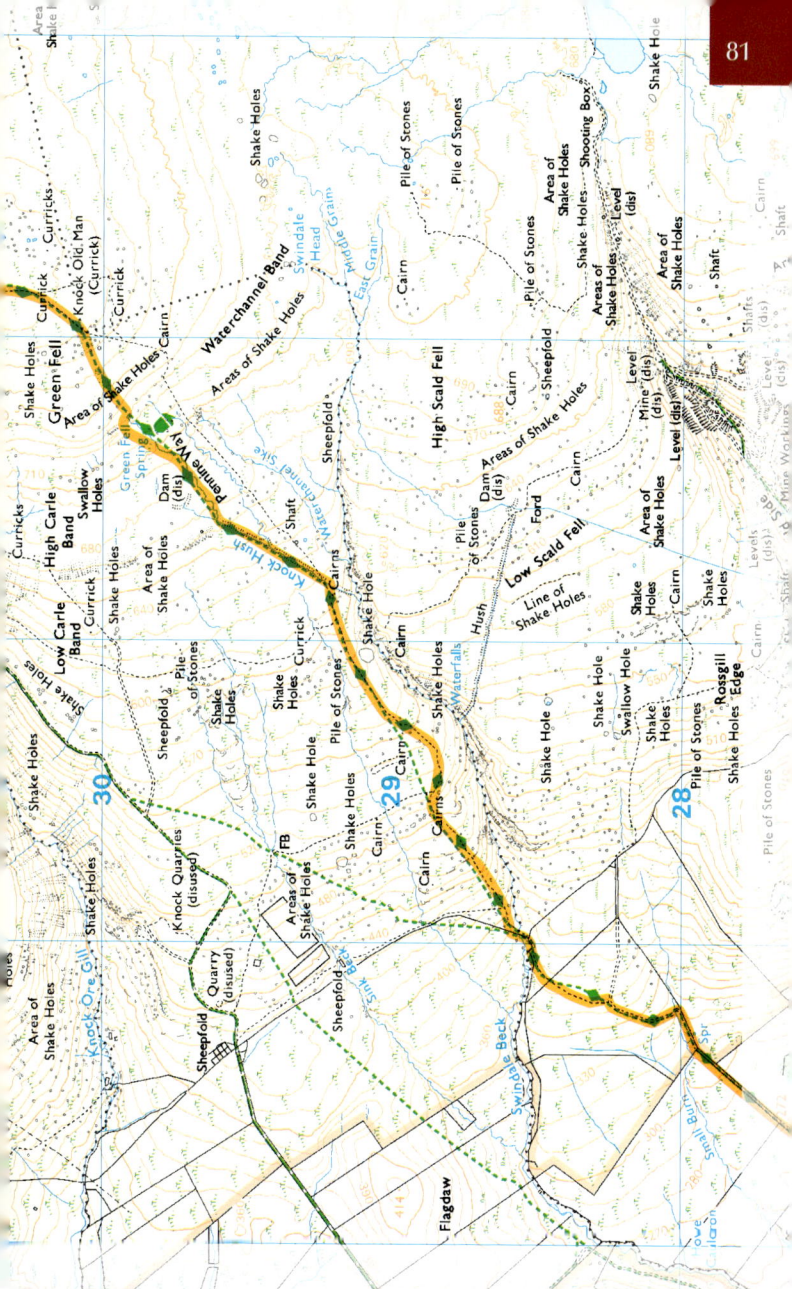

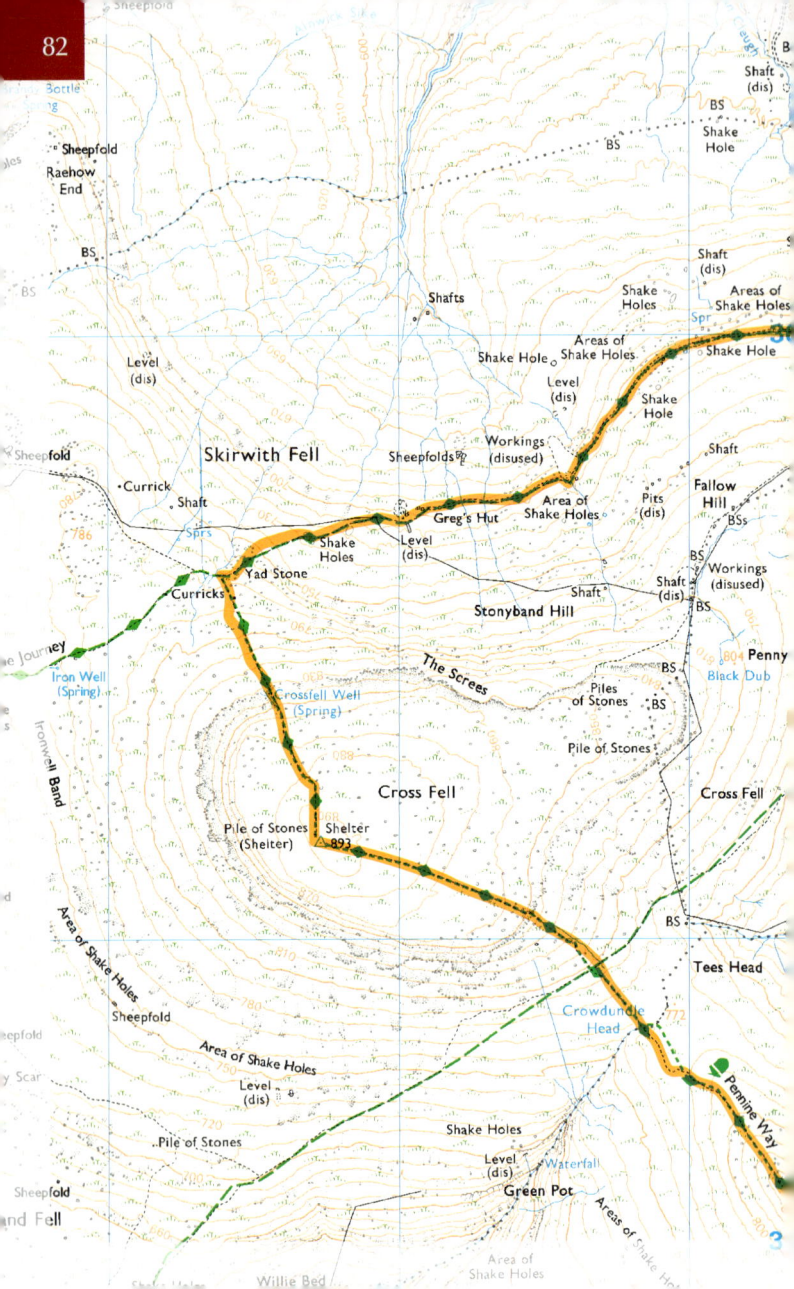

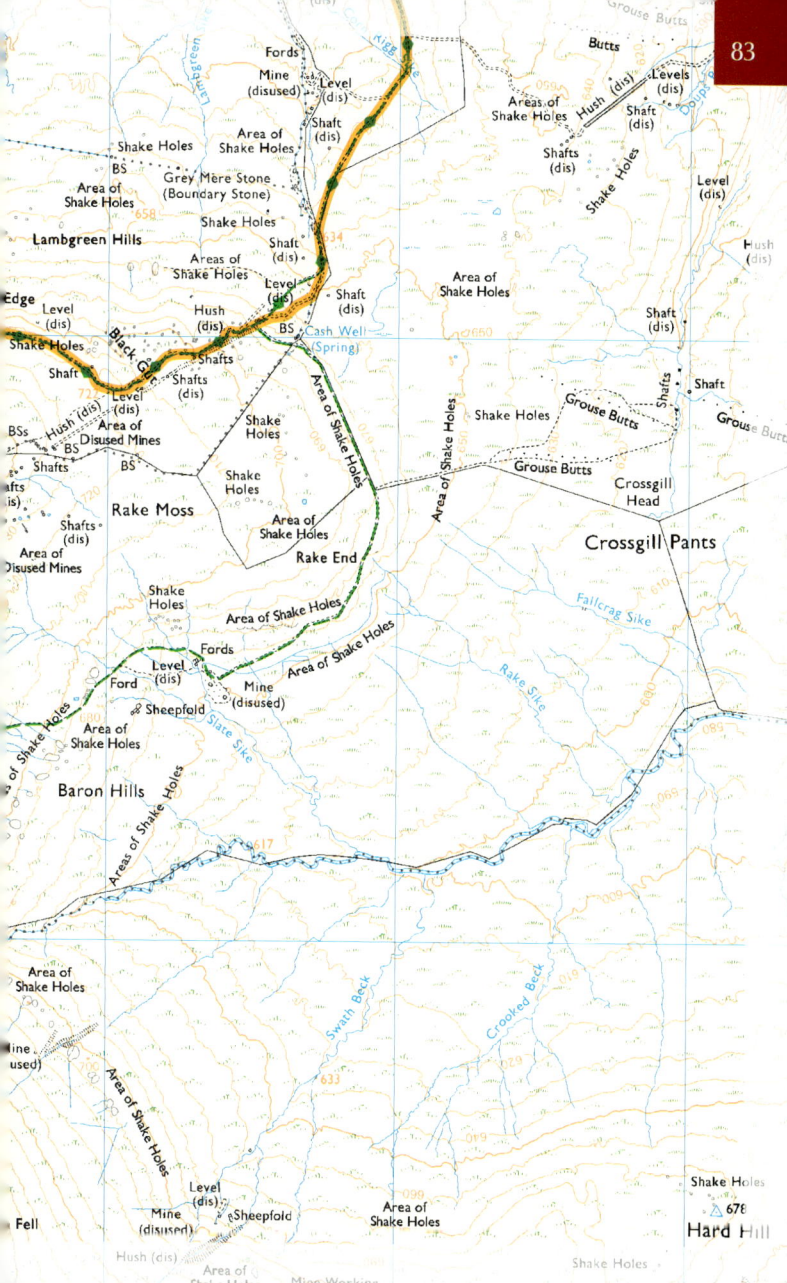

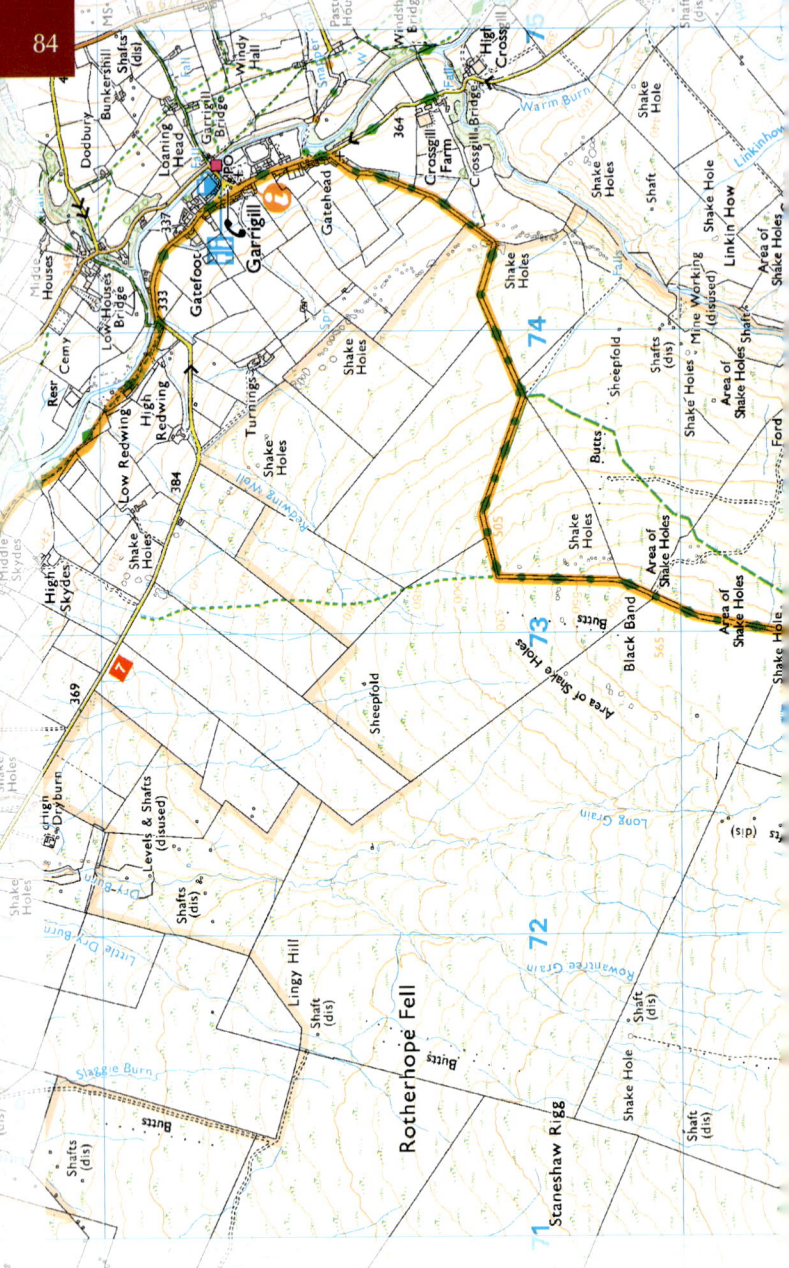

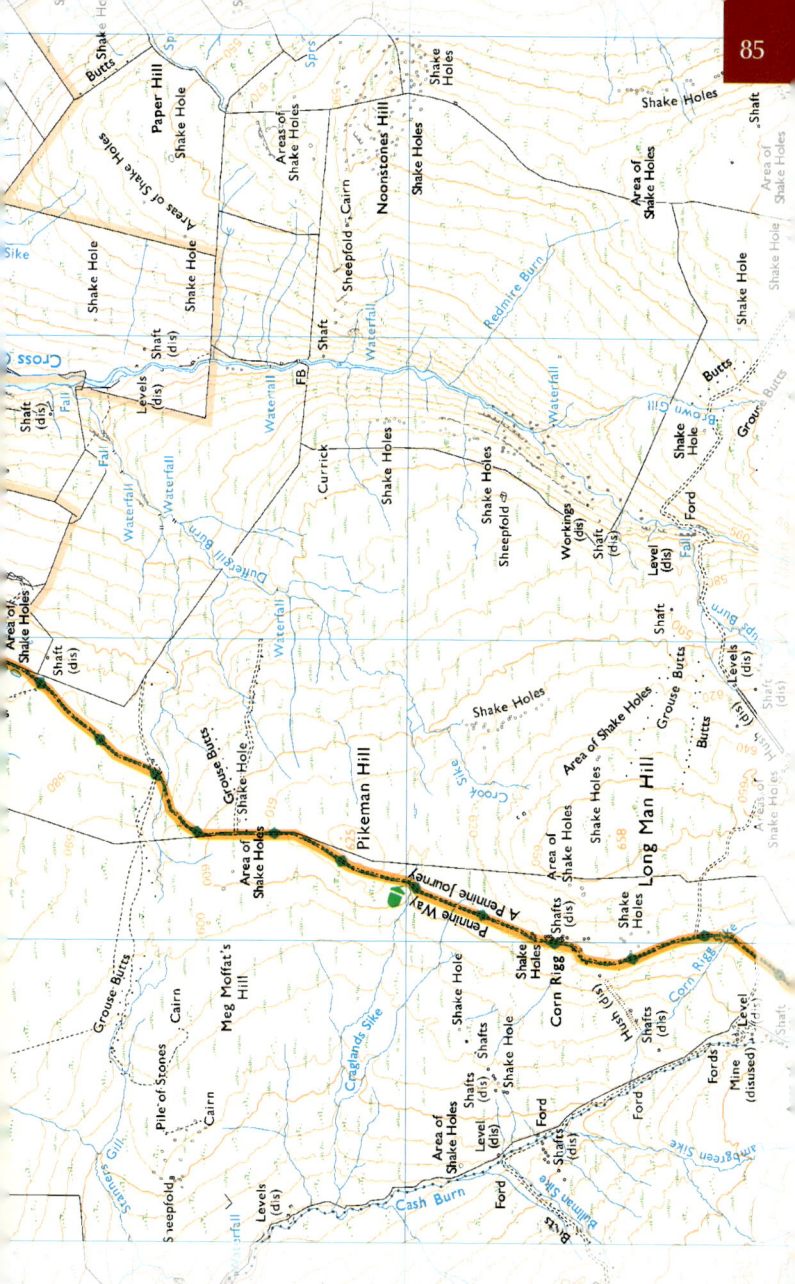

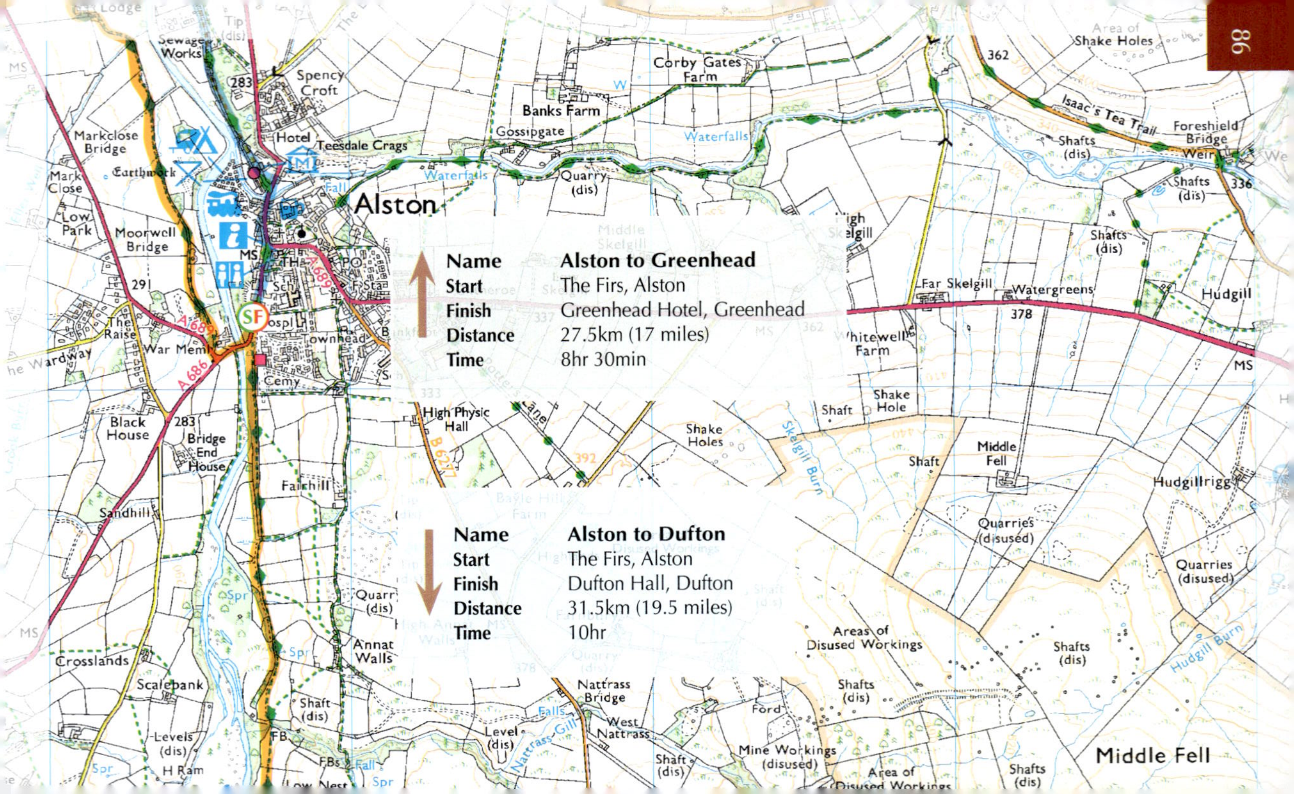

Alston to Greenhead
Name
Start The Firs, Alston
Finish Greenhead Hotel, Greenhead
Distance 27.5km (17 miles)
Time 8hr 30min

Alston to Dufton
Name
Start The Firs, Alston
Finish Dufton Hall, Dufton
Distance 31.5km (19.5 miles)
Time 10hr

88

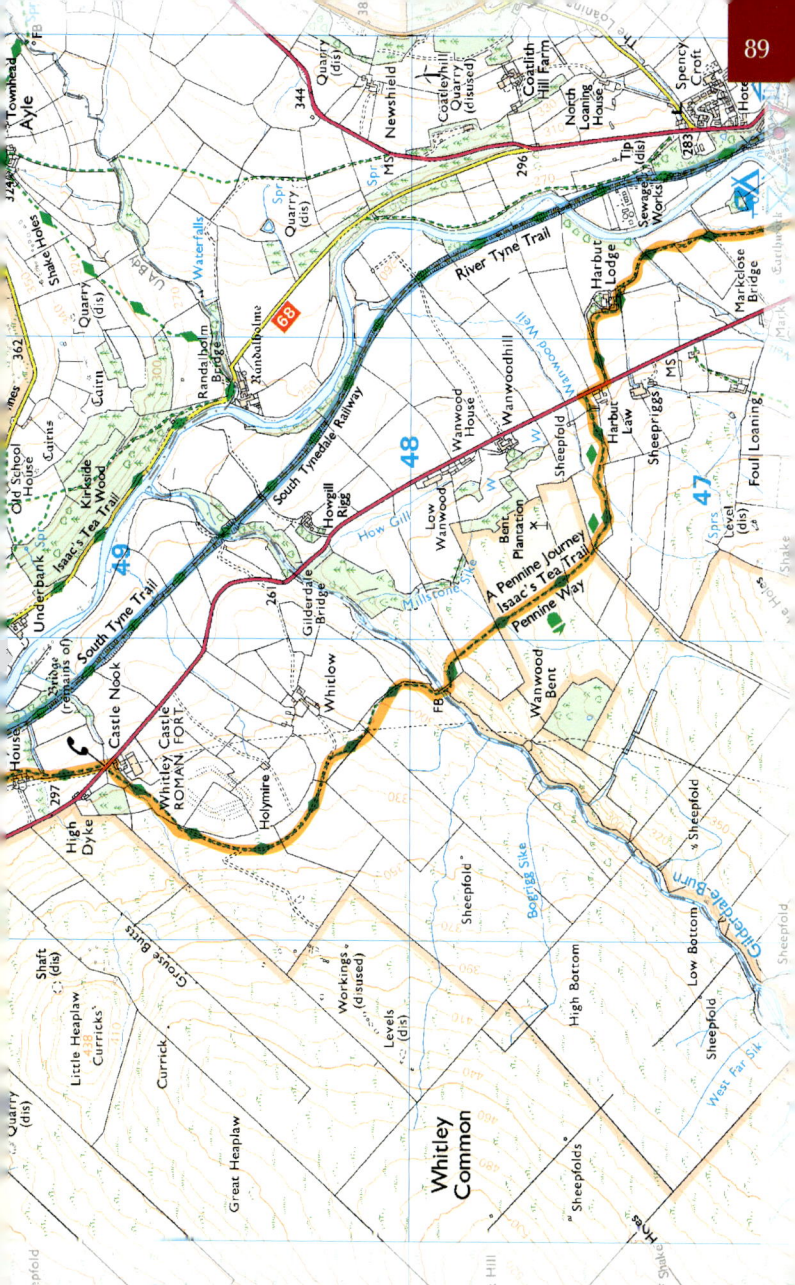

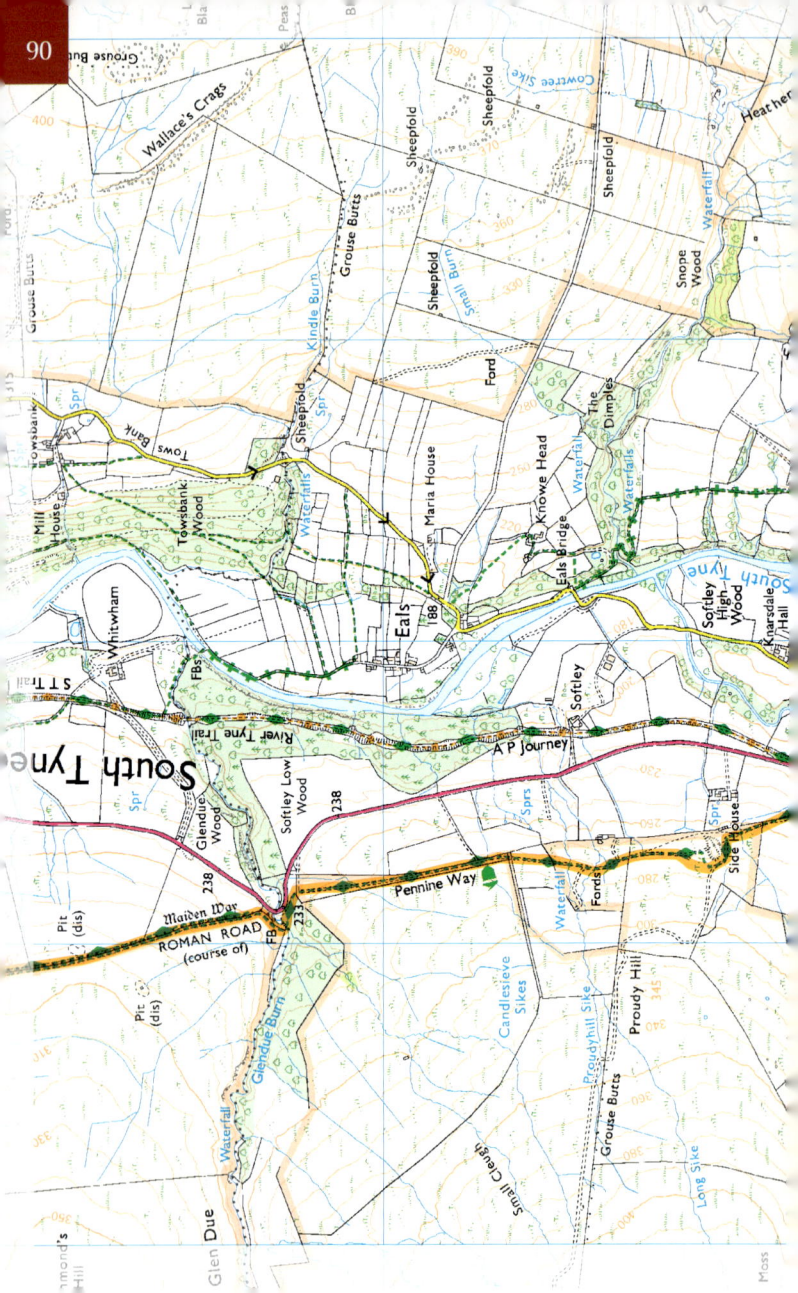

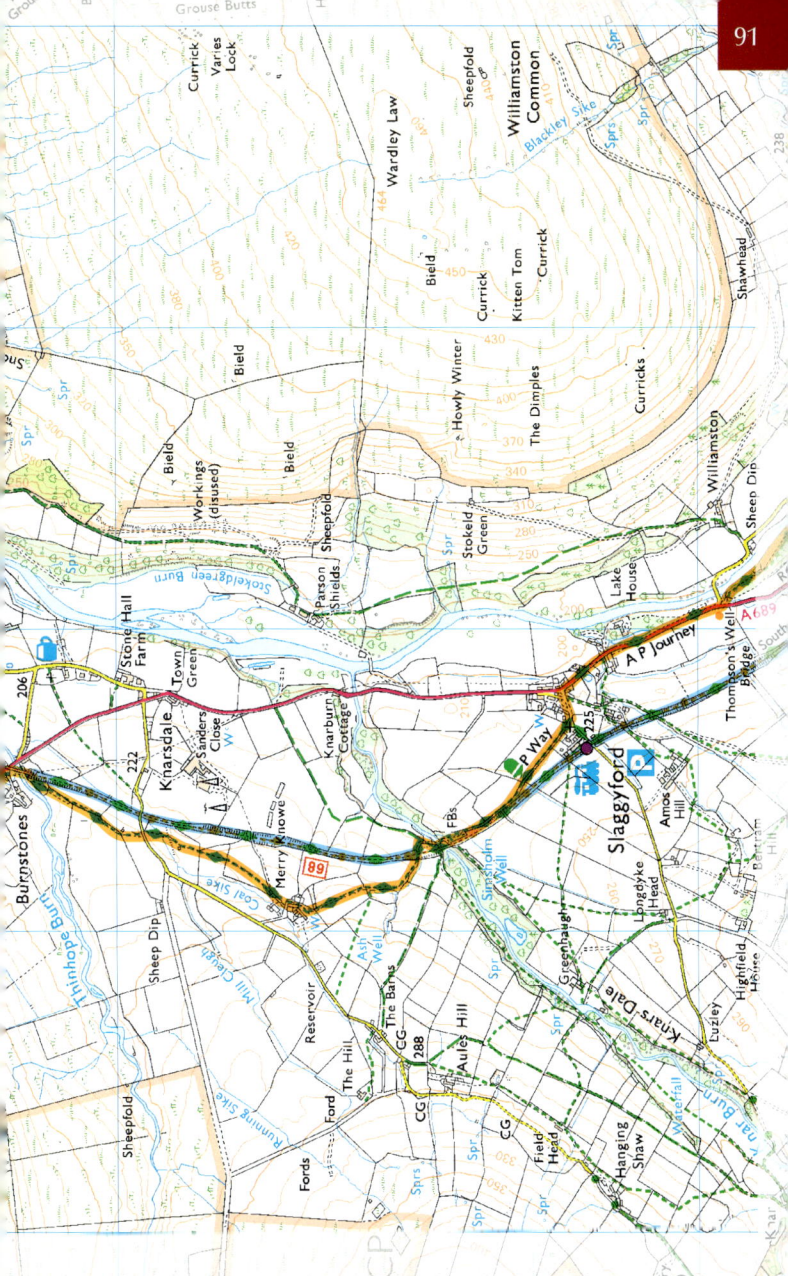

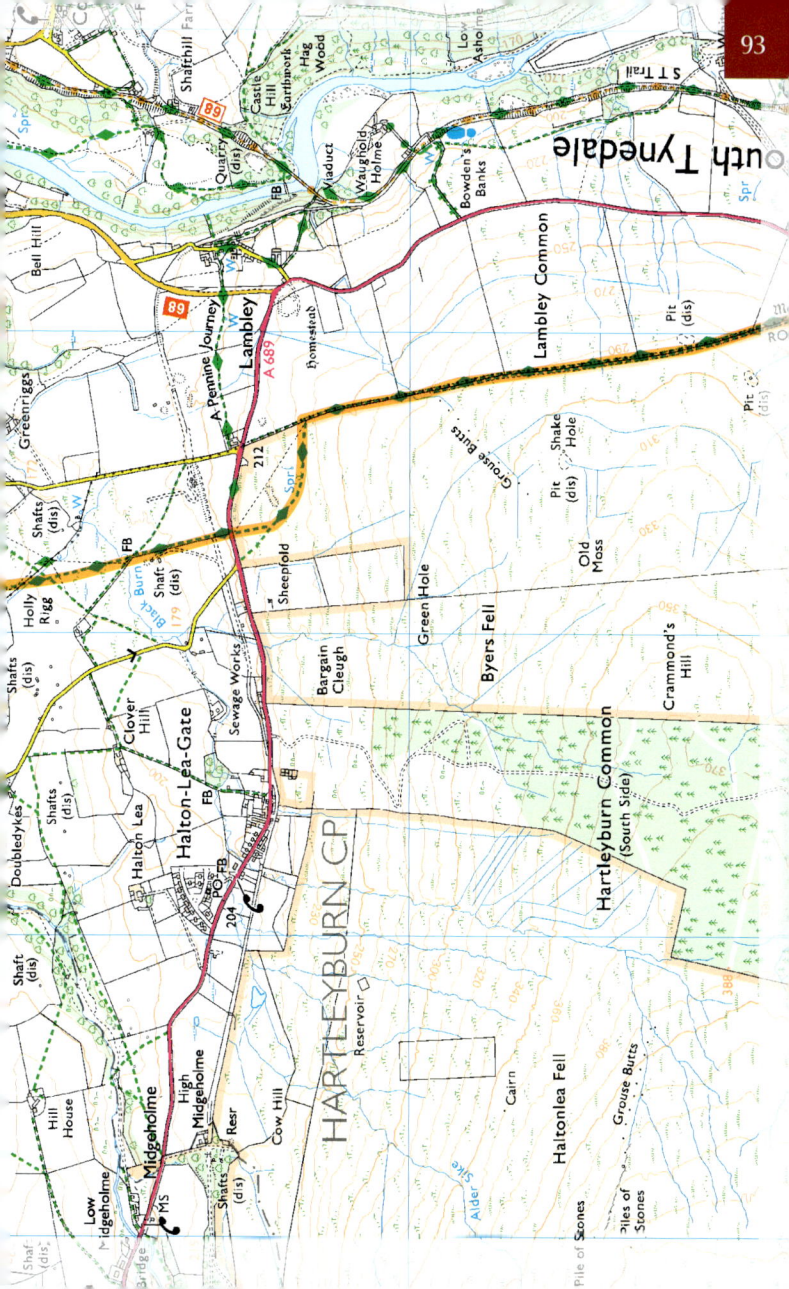

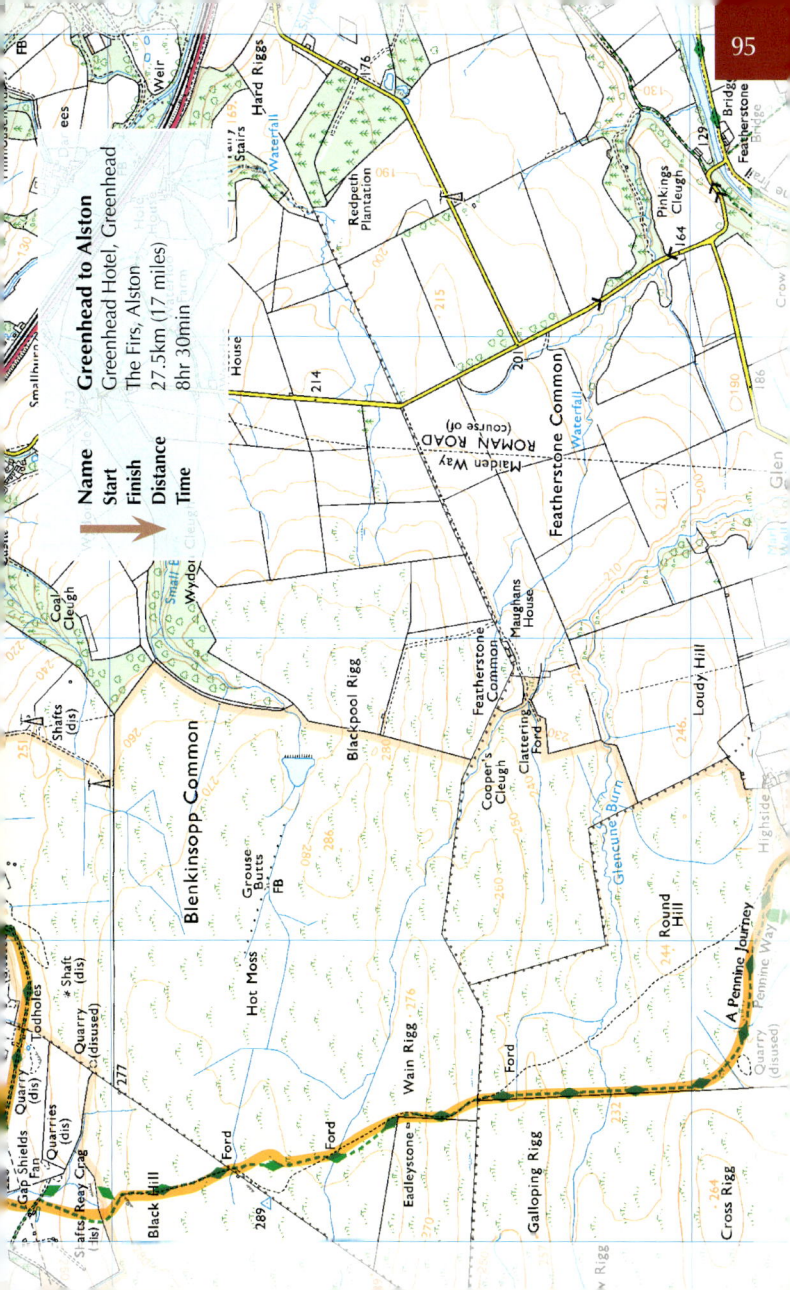

96

Inner Dodd
FBs
FB
Brown Rigg
Moss Peteral
Farglow
Tipalt Burn
Calfclose Sike
Croft Sike
Bield
Cat Cleugh
Low Tipalt
Ford
CG
Waterfall
CG
Dowy Scar
CG
Hangingshields Rigg
FBs
High Old Shields
FB
North Plantation
CG
Collar Heugh Crag
Allolee Rigg
GREENHEAD CP
HADRIAN'S WALL
TURRET 44A
MILECASTLE 44
Workings (disused)
TURRET 44B
ROMAN MILITARY WAY
TURRE
FB
Walltown Crags
King Arthur's Well
Alloa Lea
MILECASTLE 45
CG
Walltown
VALLUM (course of)
Quarry (dis)
CG
TURRET 45A
Lowtown
CG
VALLUM
Spr
Blake Law
TURRET 45B
CG
Peat Steel
HALTW
Walltown Wood
Fellend Moss
Dintley Hill
Quarry (disused)
Peatsteel Crags
Haltwhistle Common
Stanegate
Shaft (dis)
ROMAN CAMP
Roman Army Museum
ROMAN ROAD (course of)
Adit (dis)
Fell End
Greenwood
Shaft
Painsdale B
Hardriggs
Wrytree

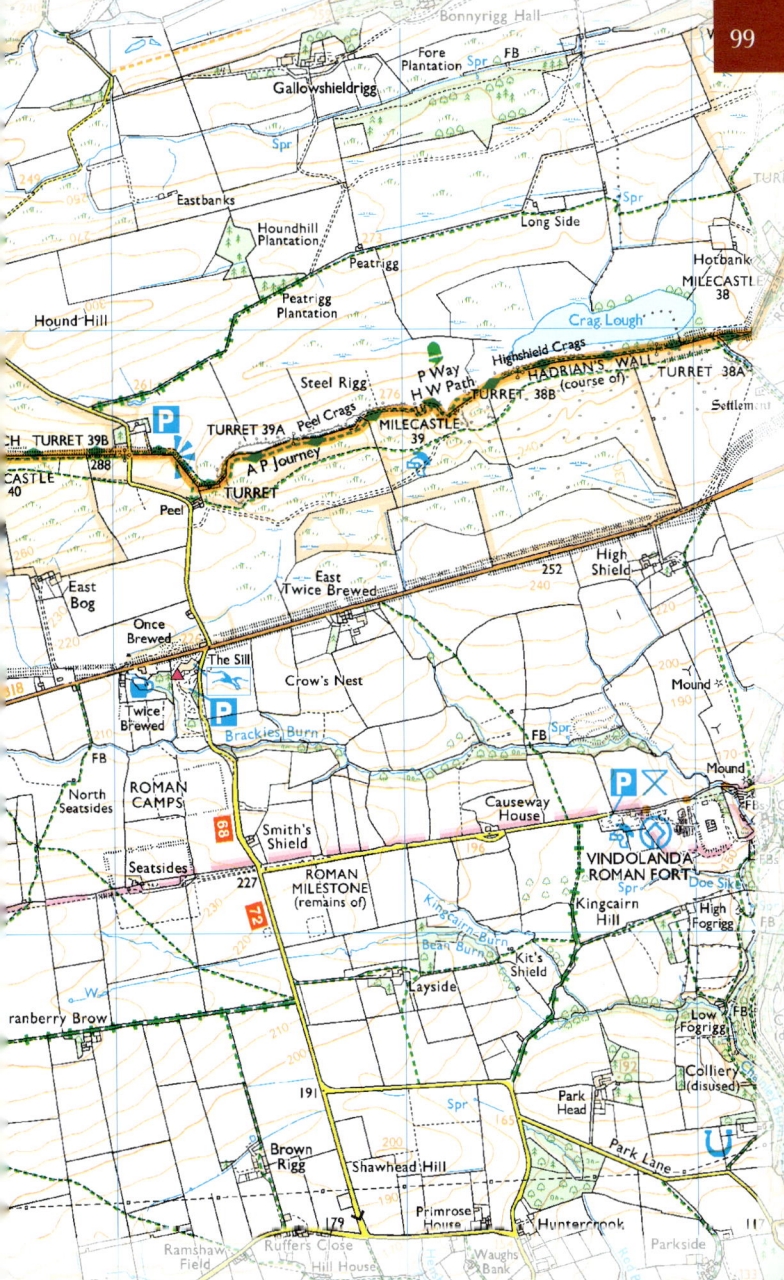

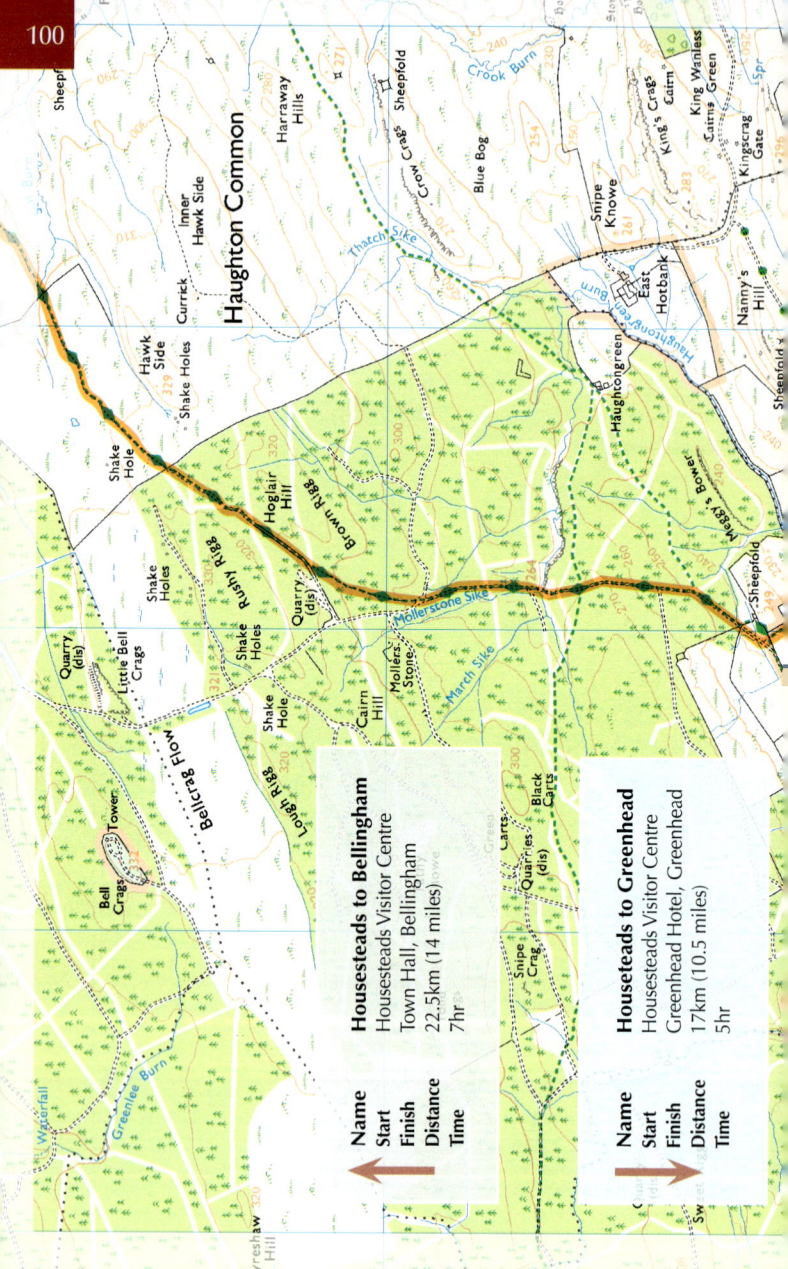

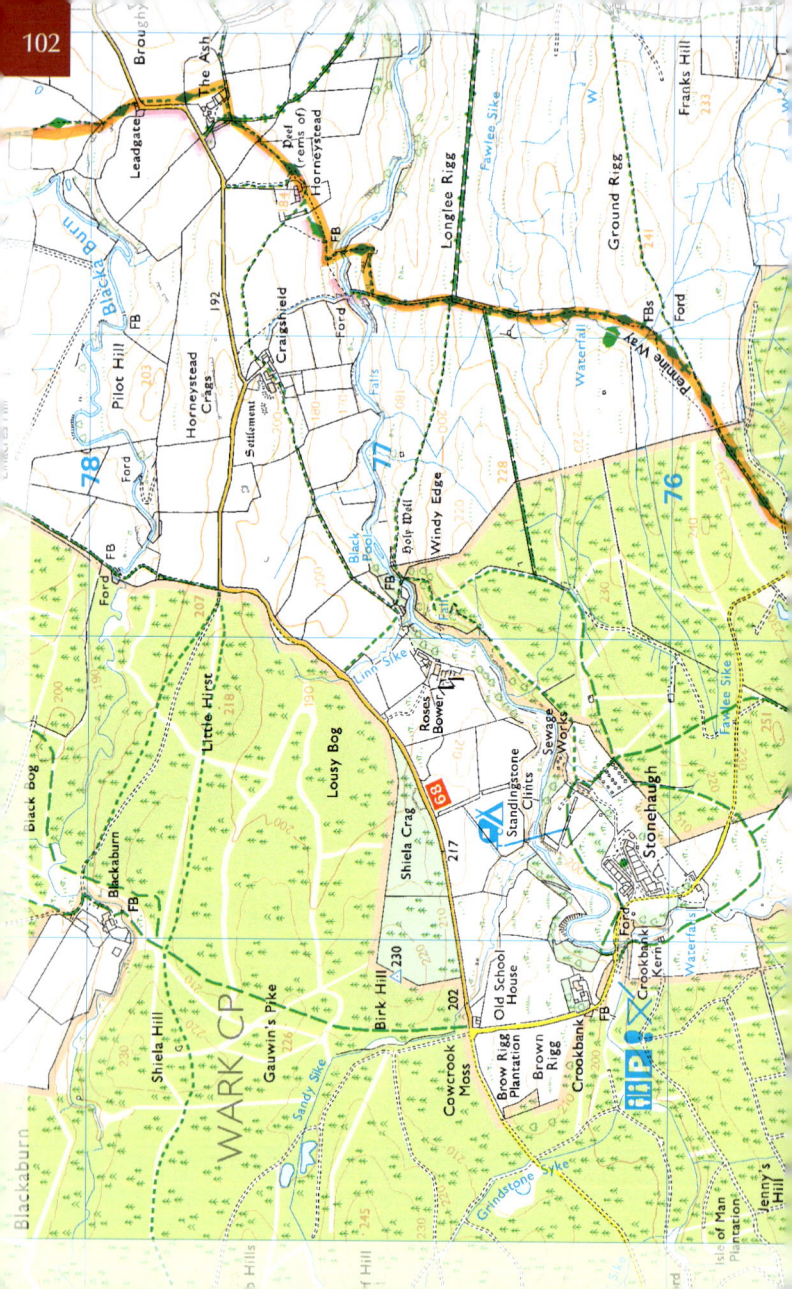

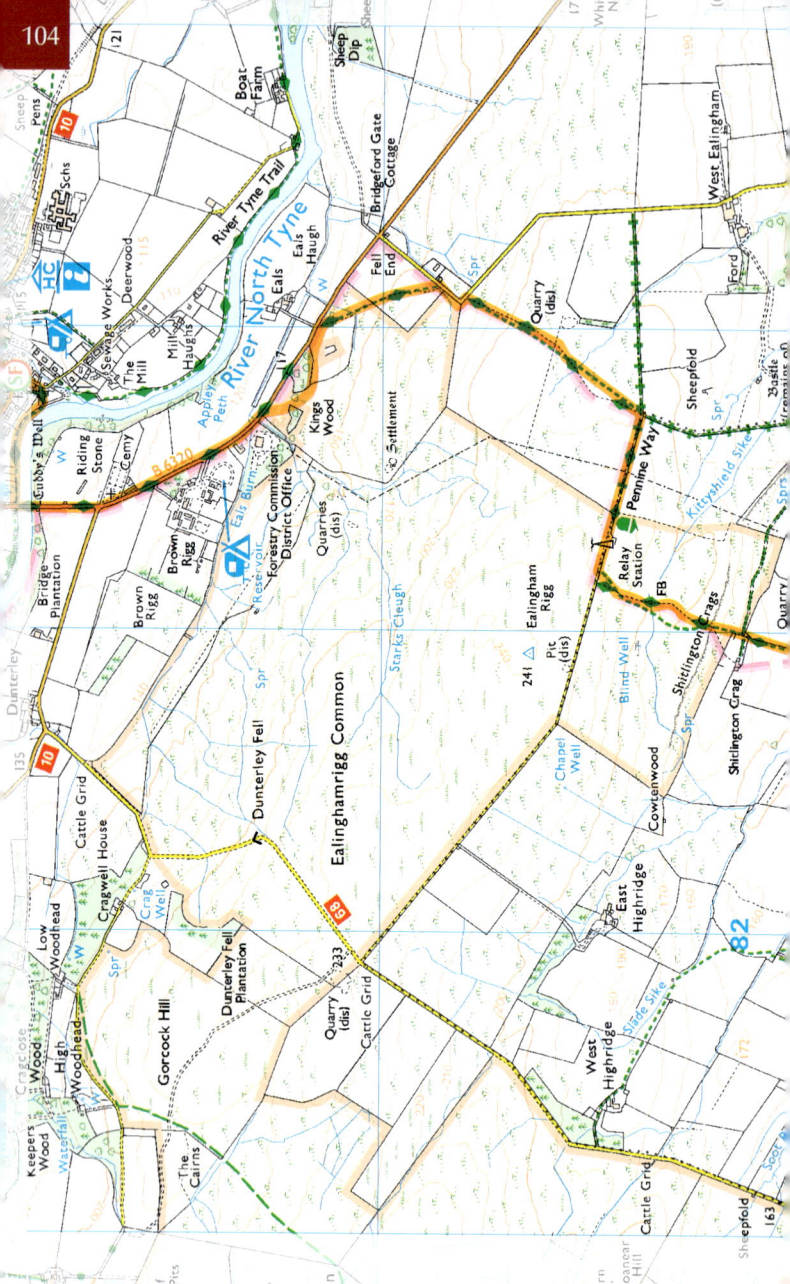

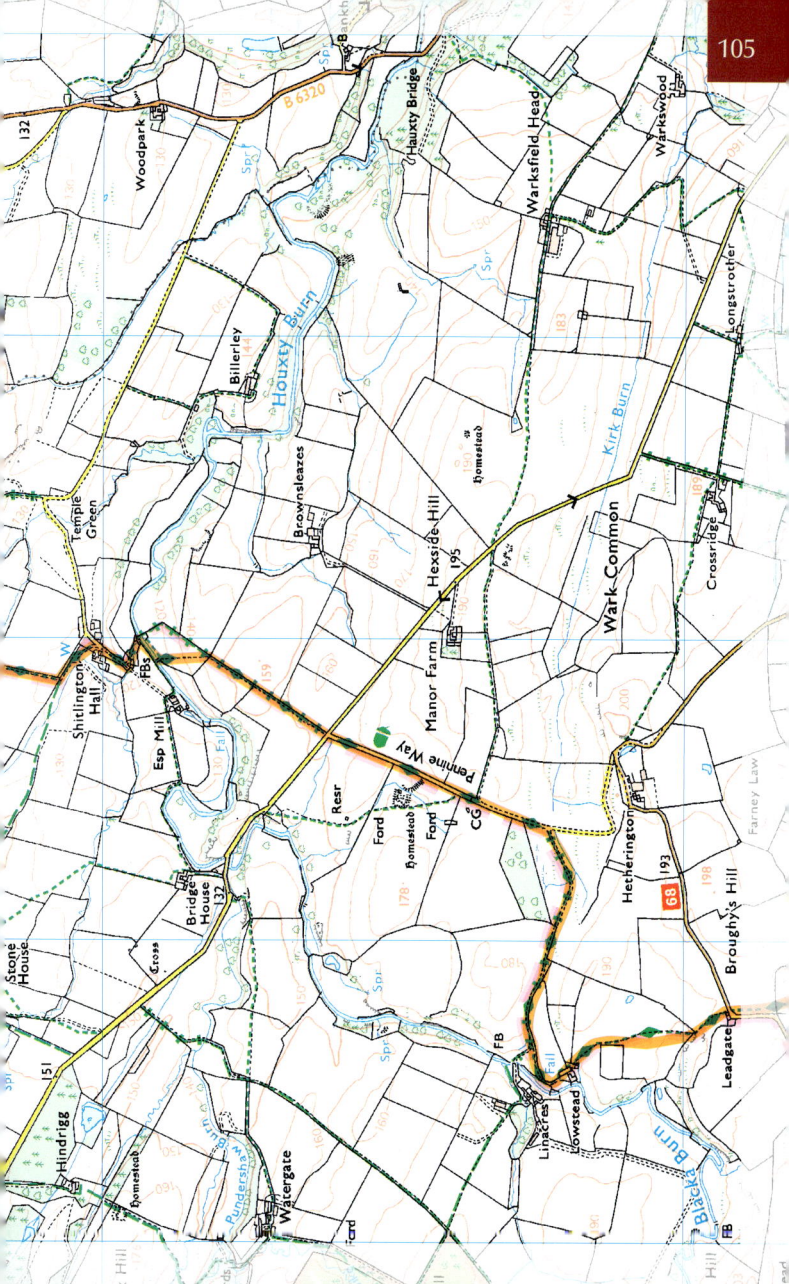

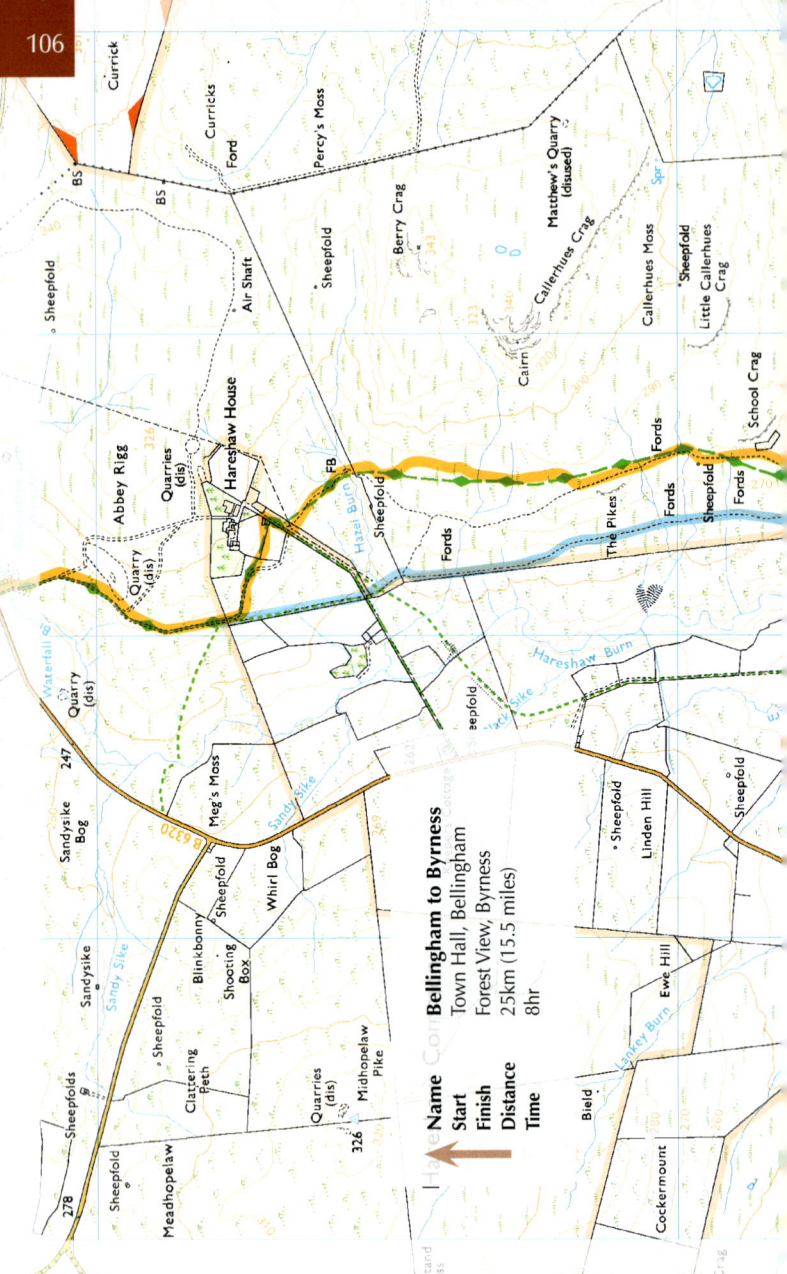

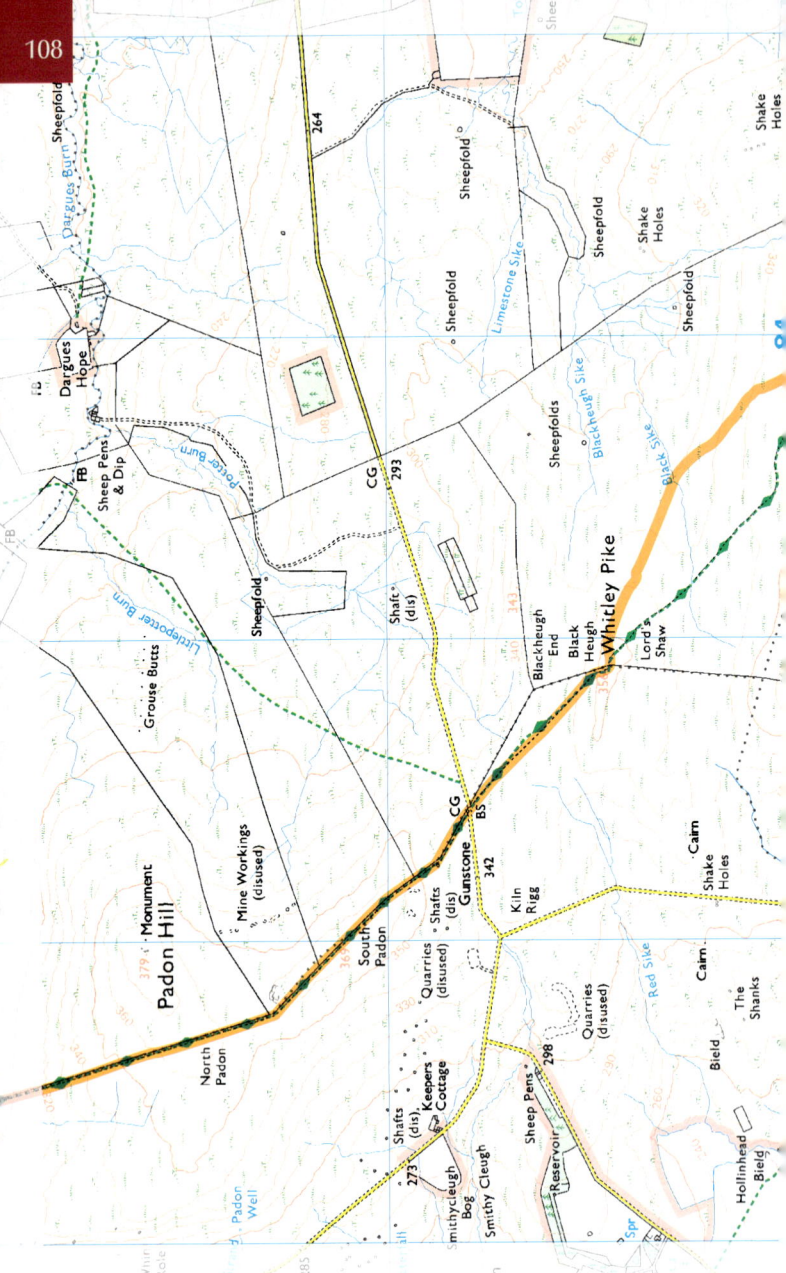

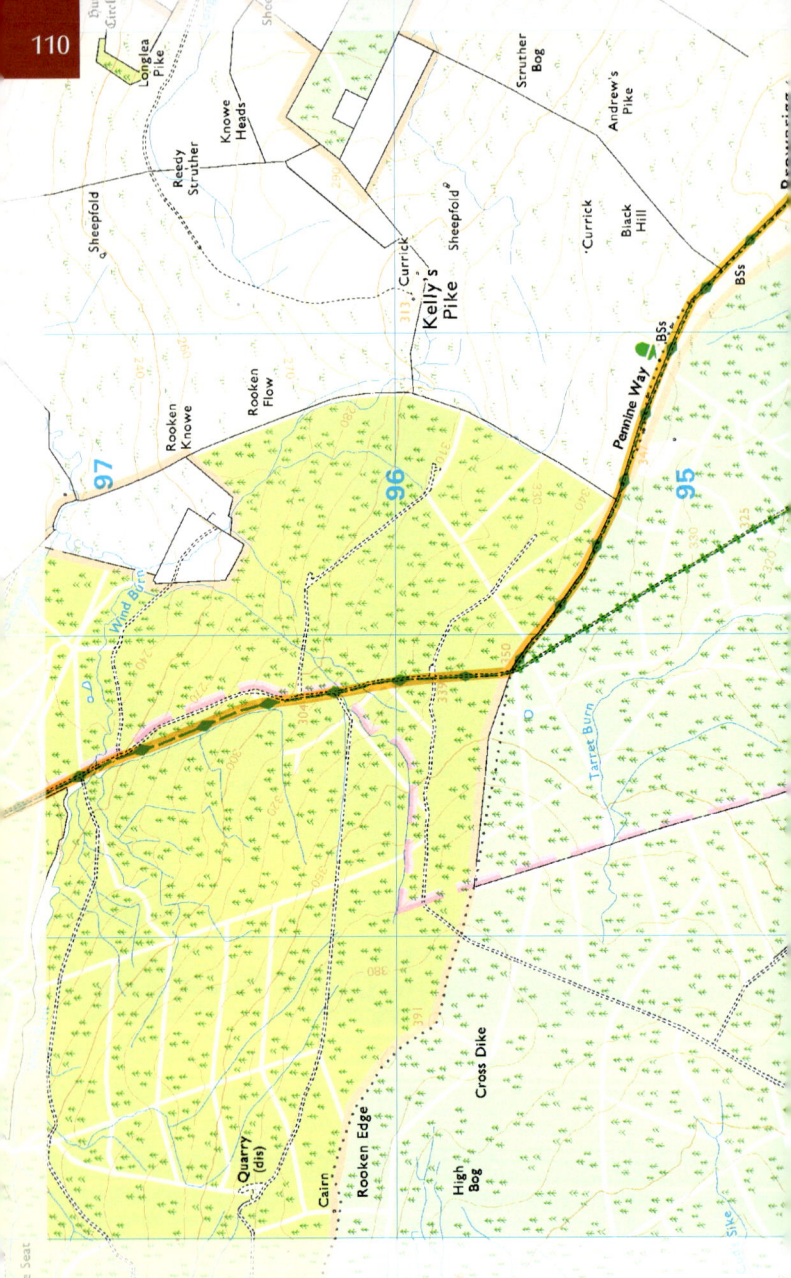

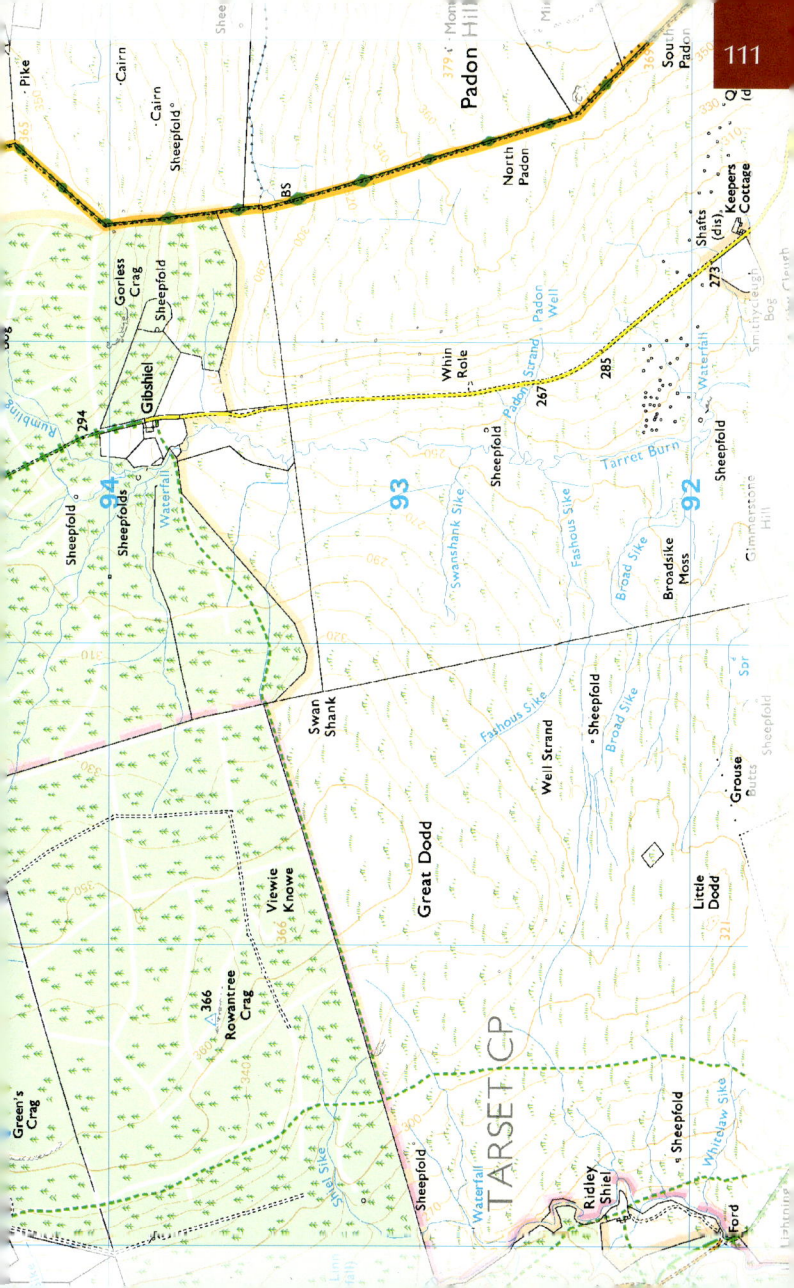

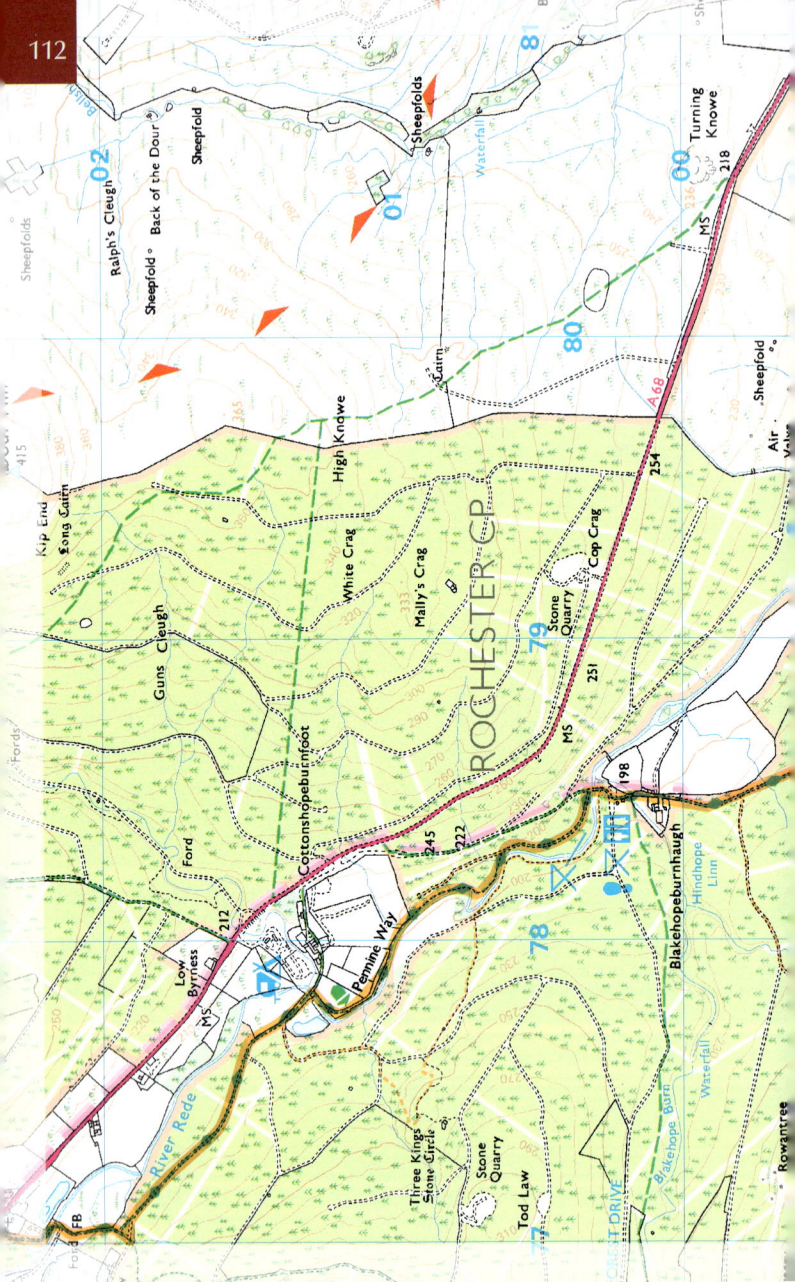

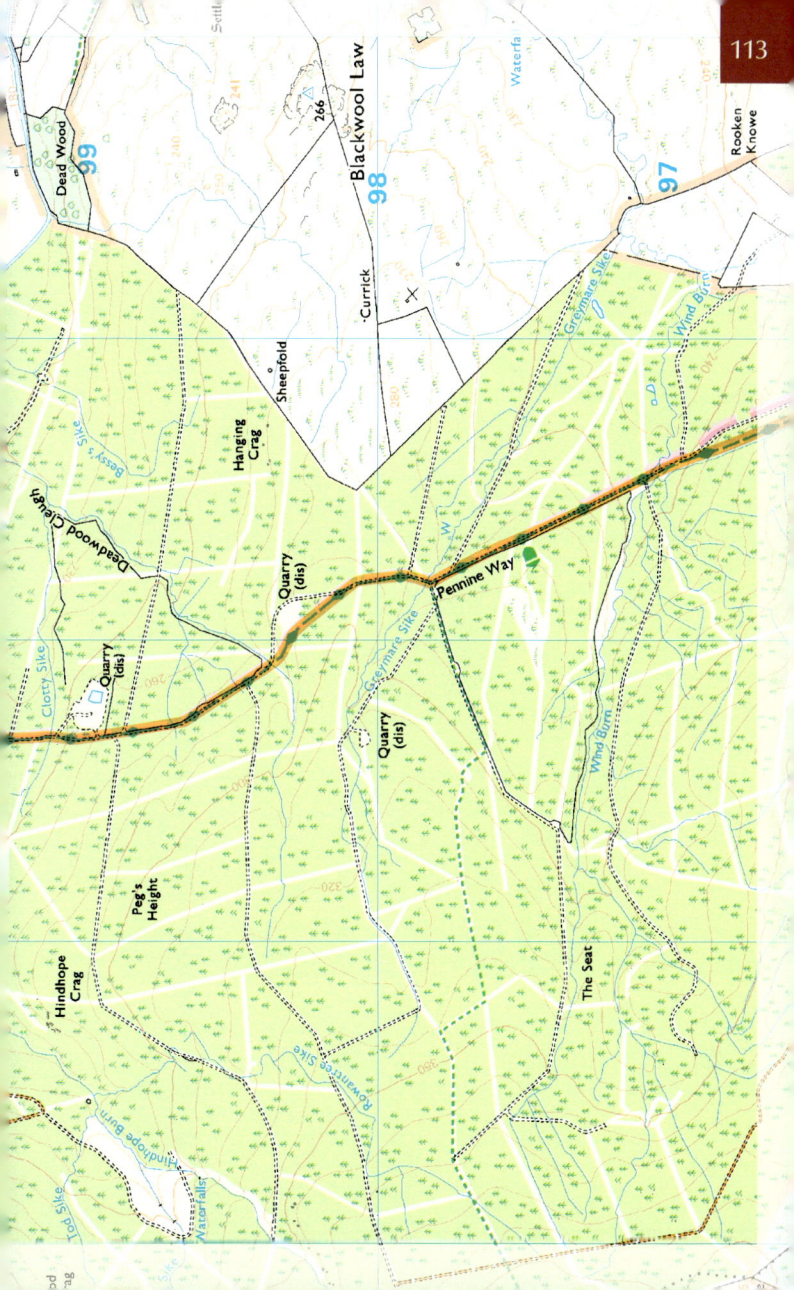

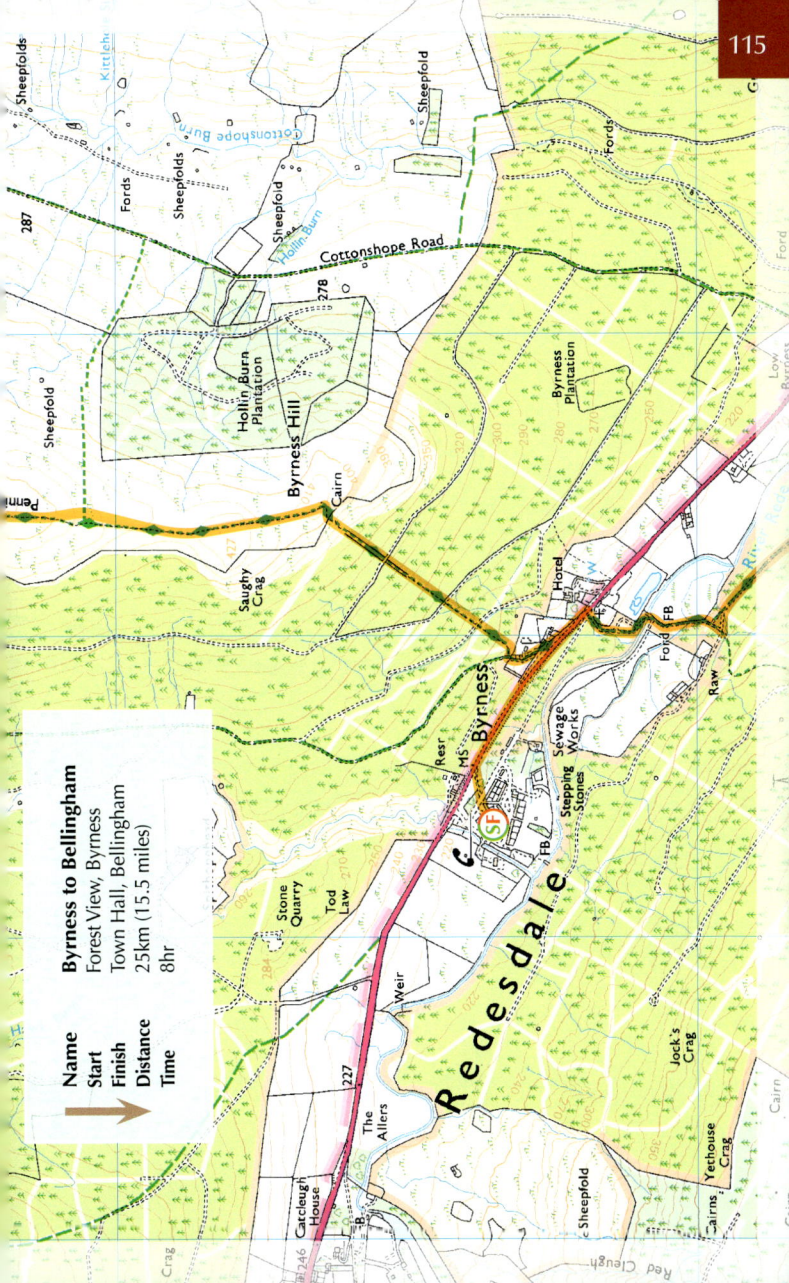

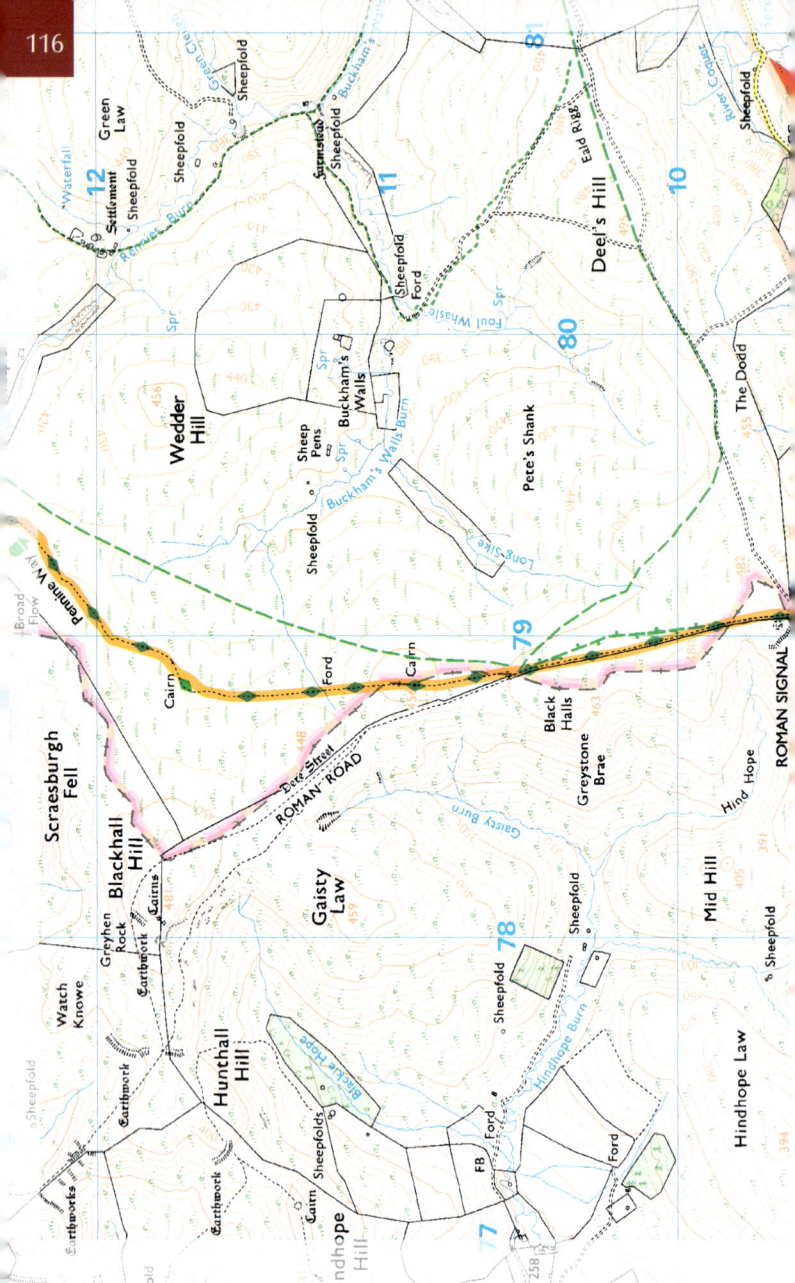

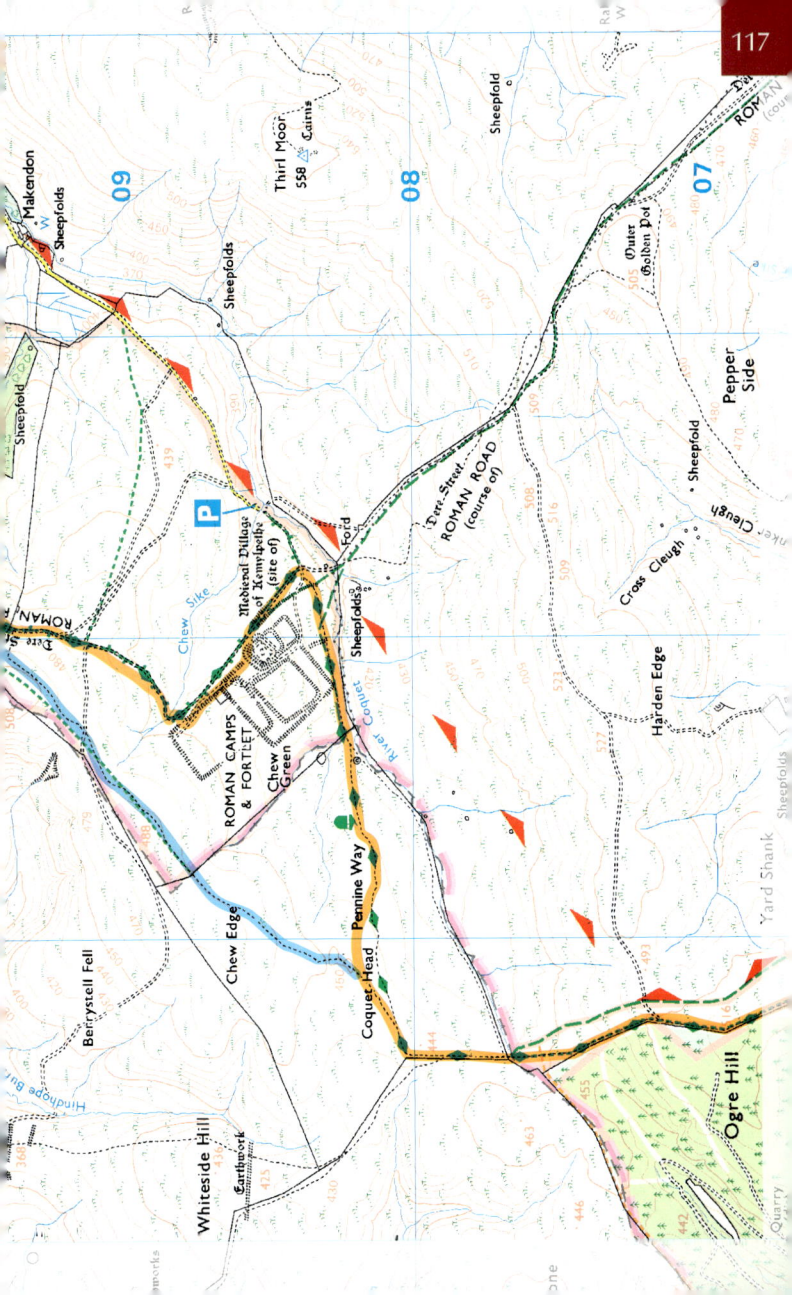

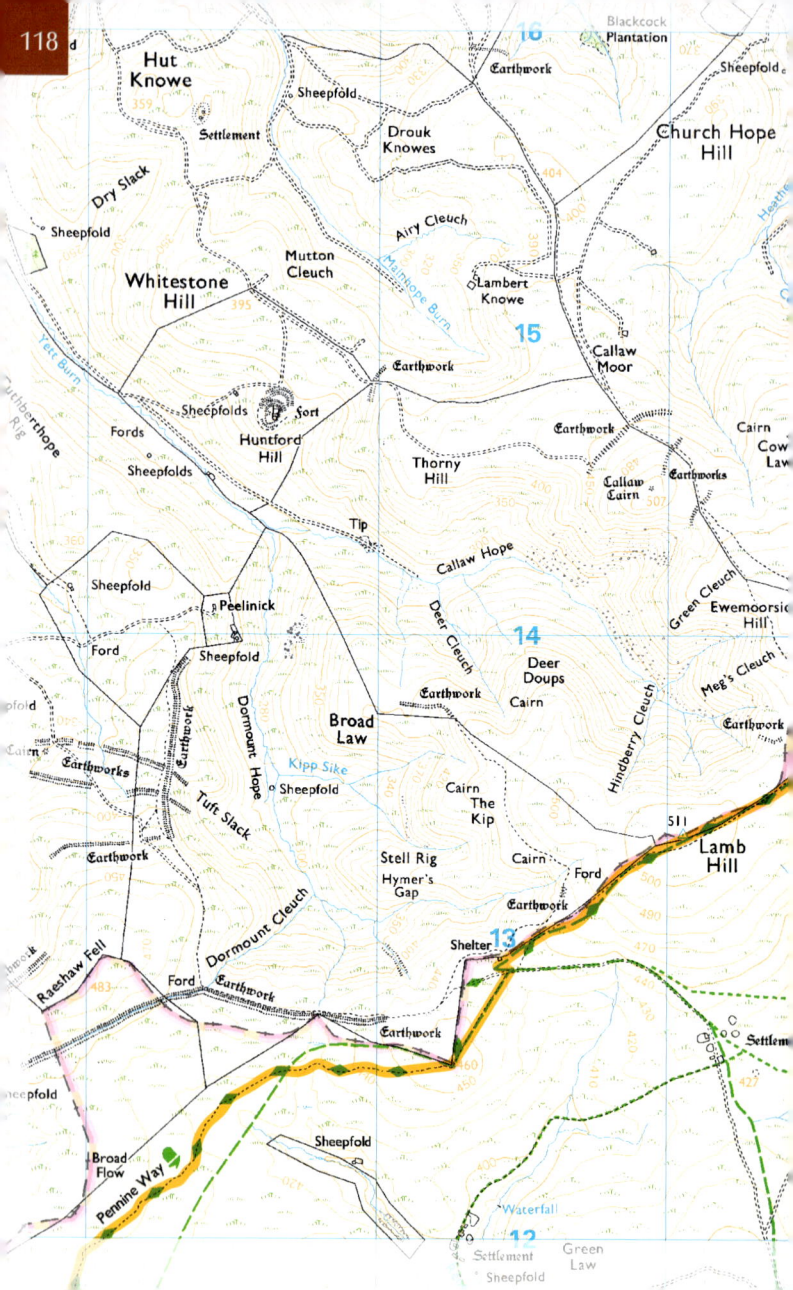

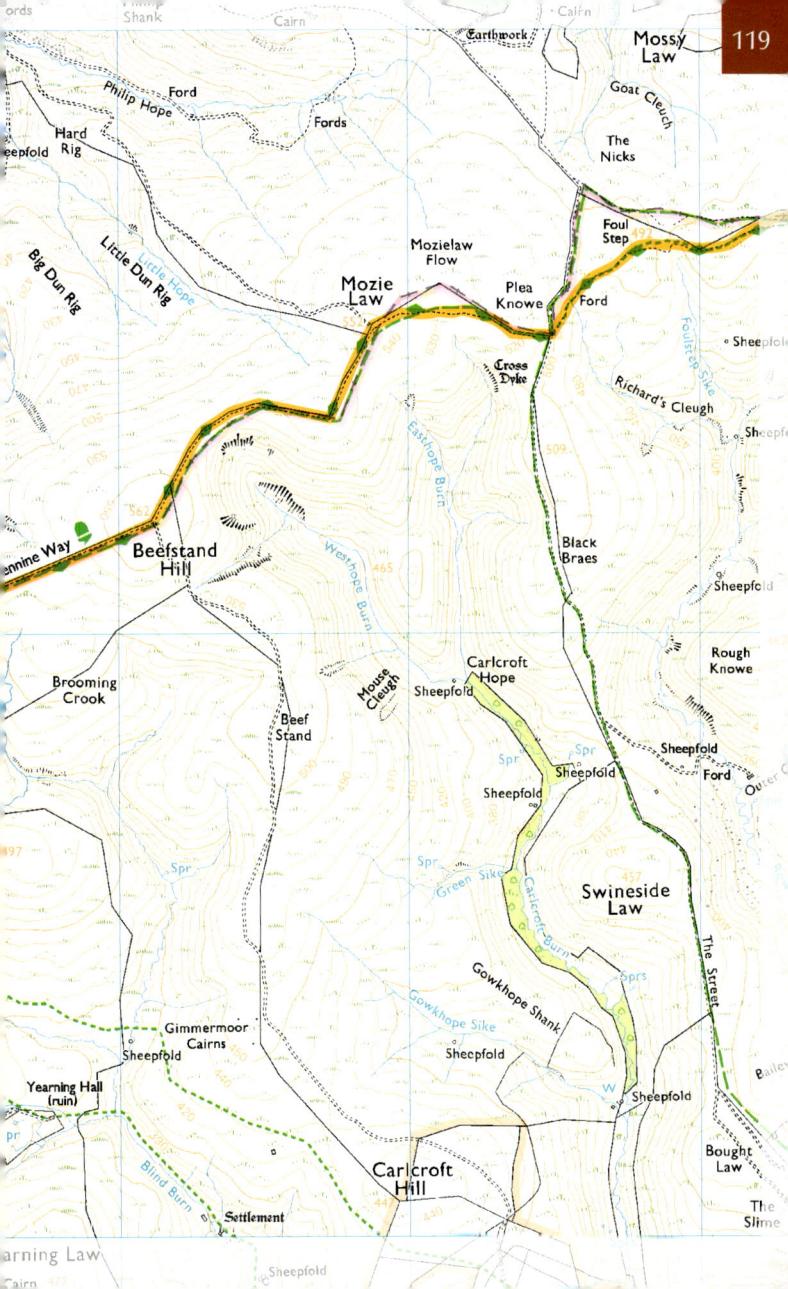

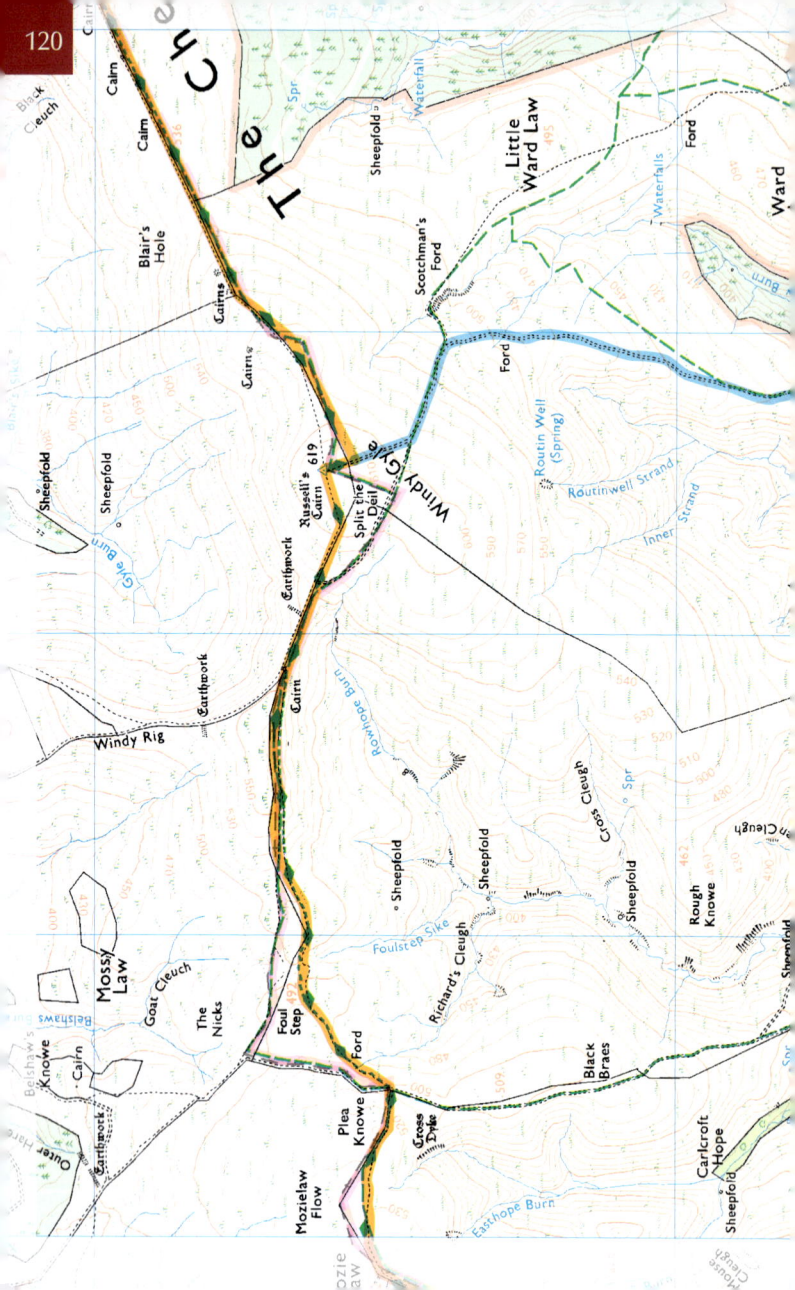

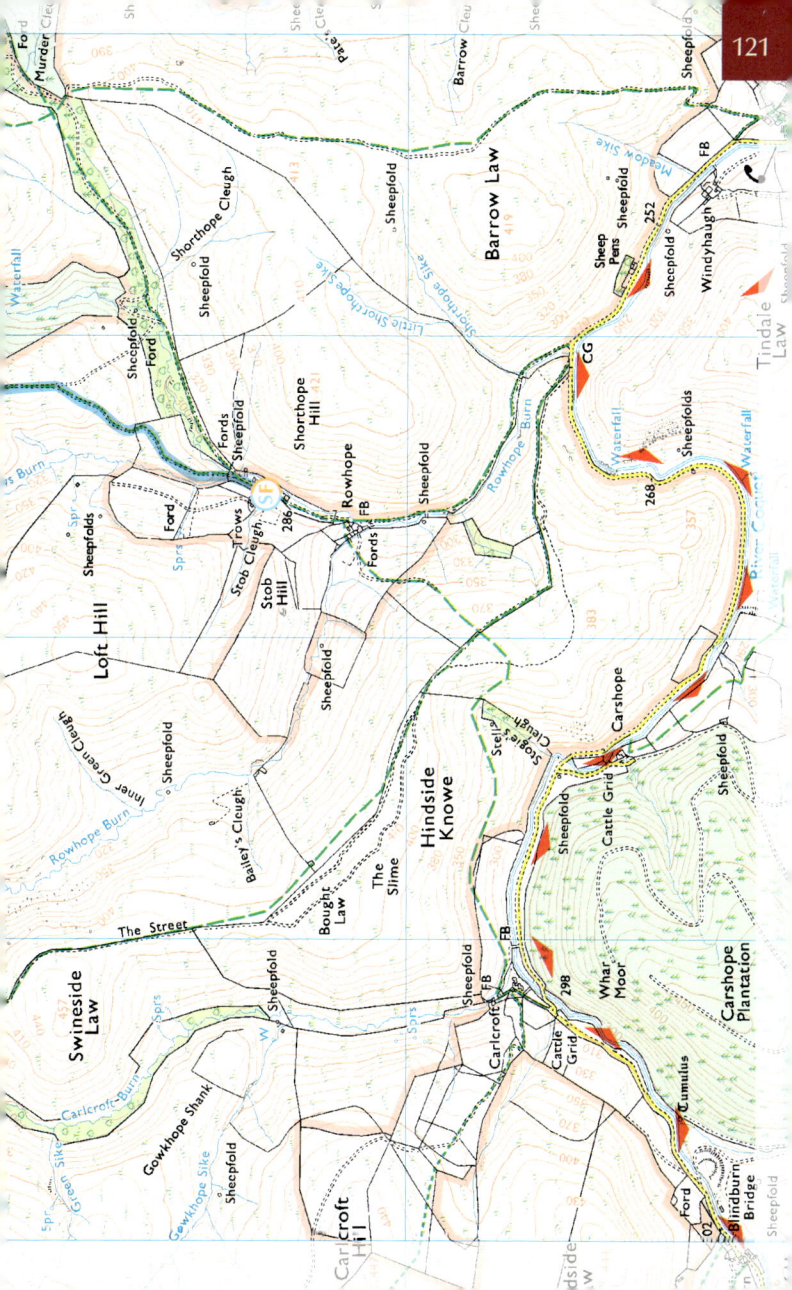

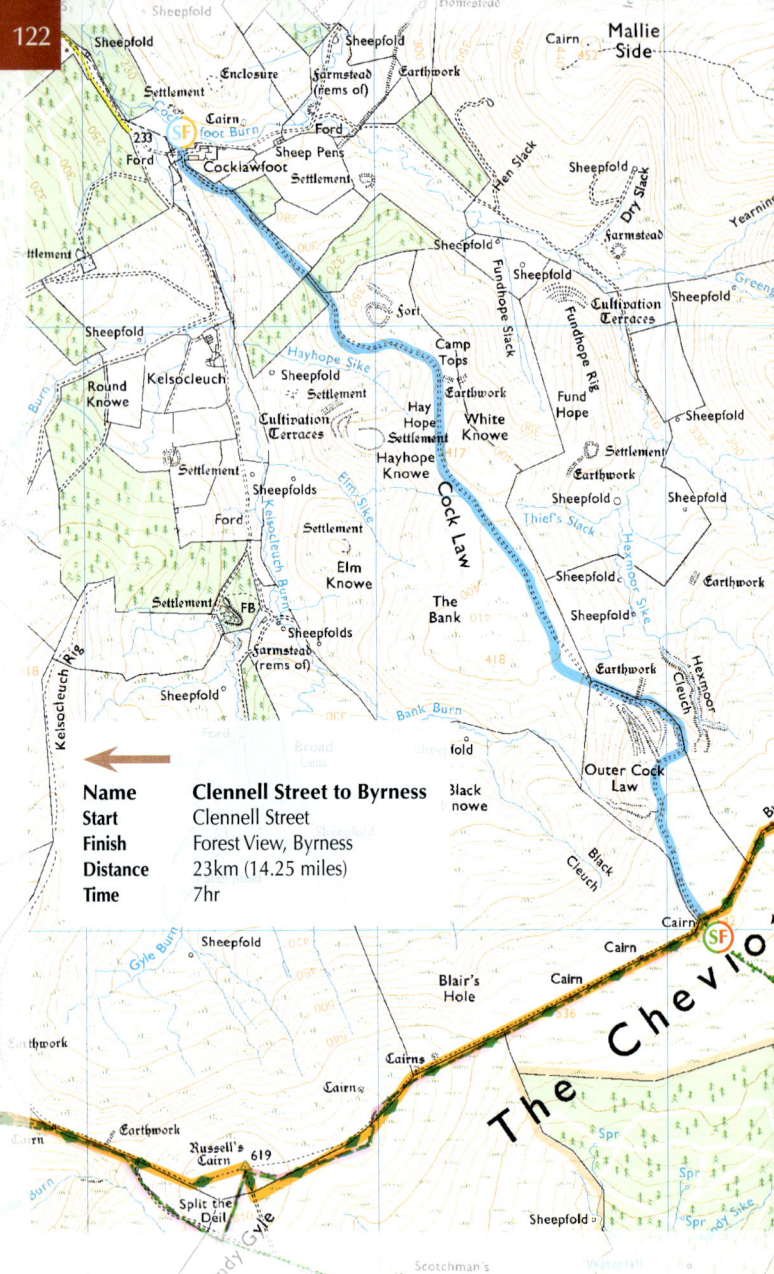

Name	**Clennell Street to Byrness**
Start	Clennell Street
Finish	Forest View, Byrness
Distance	23km (14.25 miles)
Time	7hr

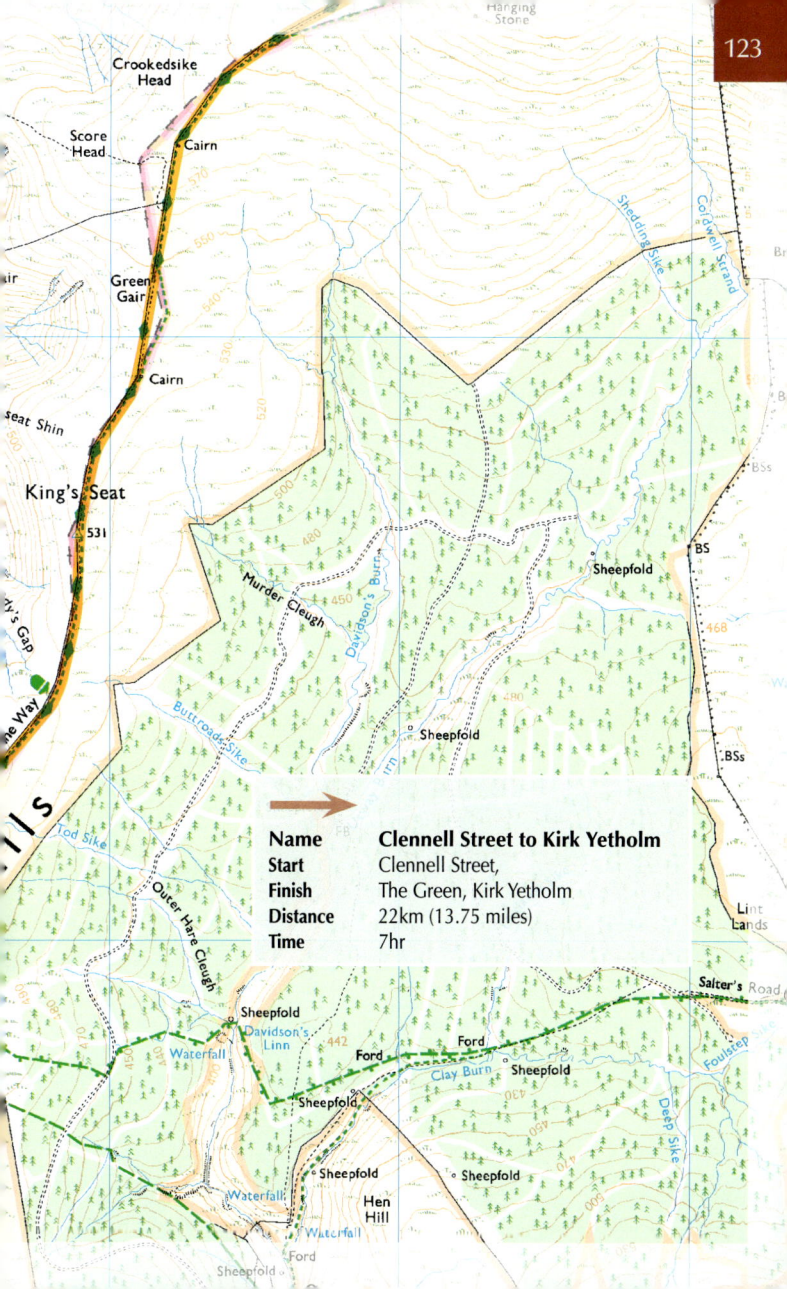

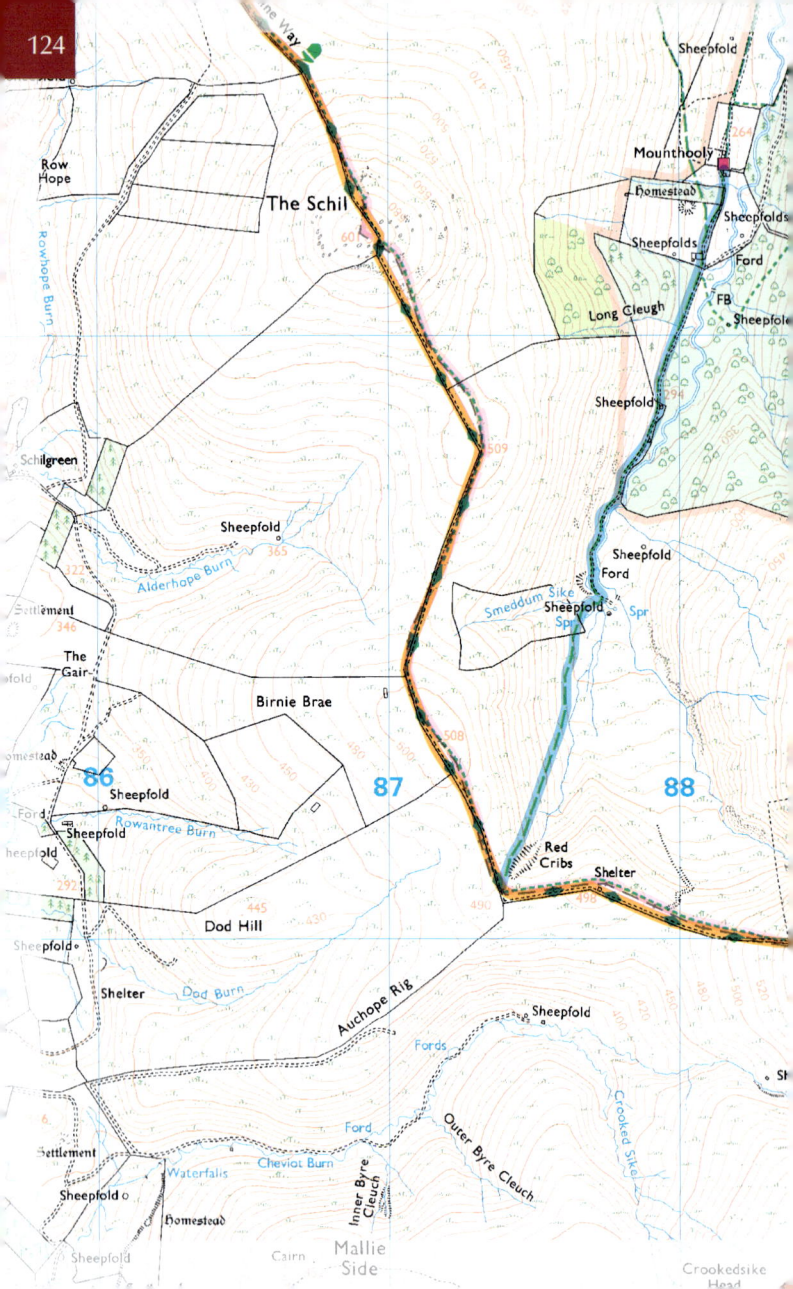

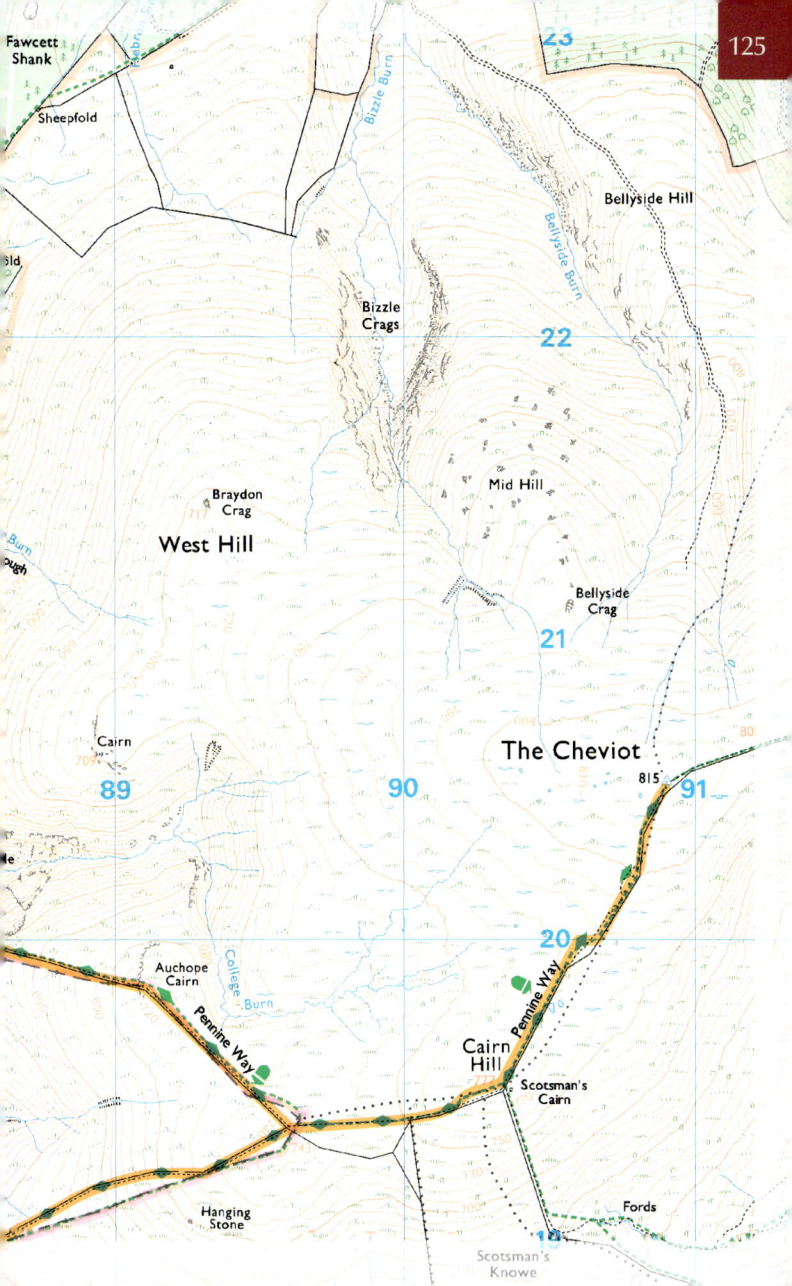

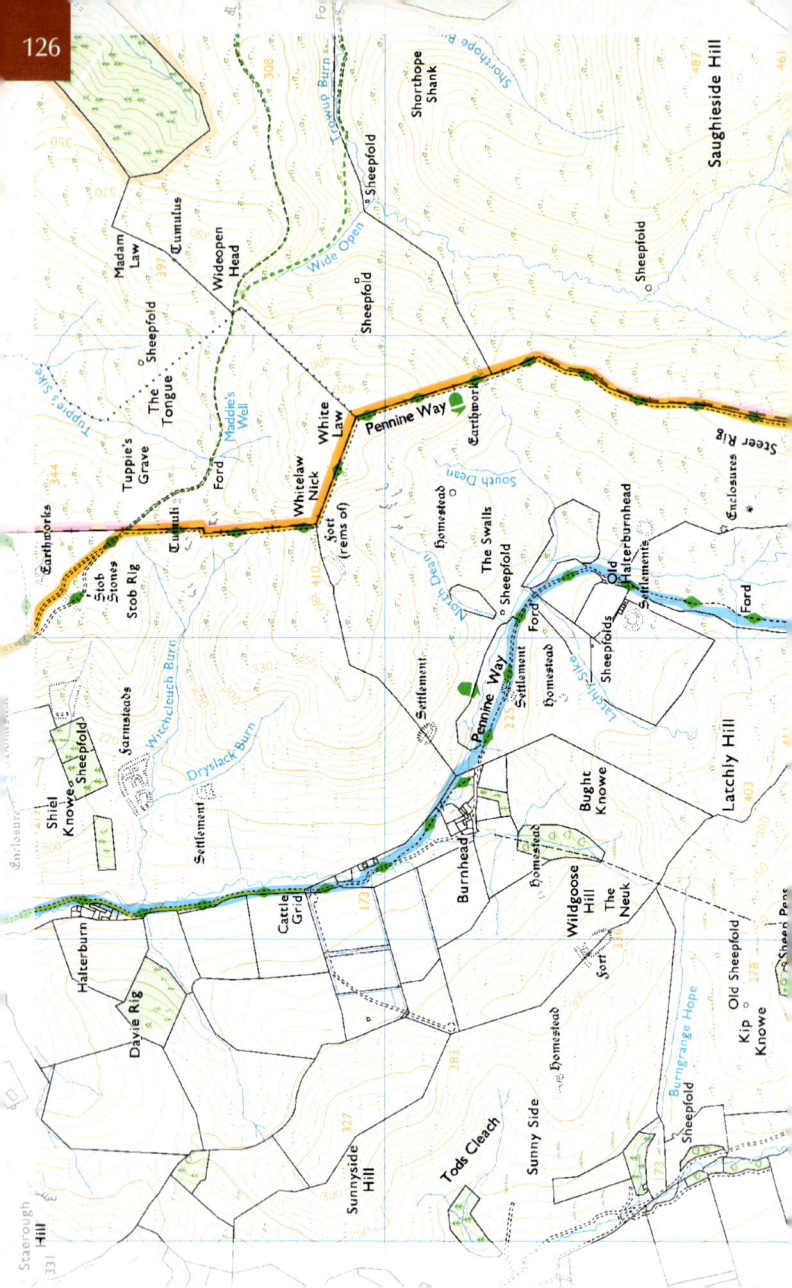

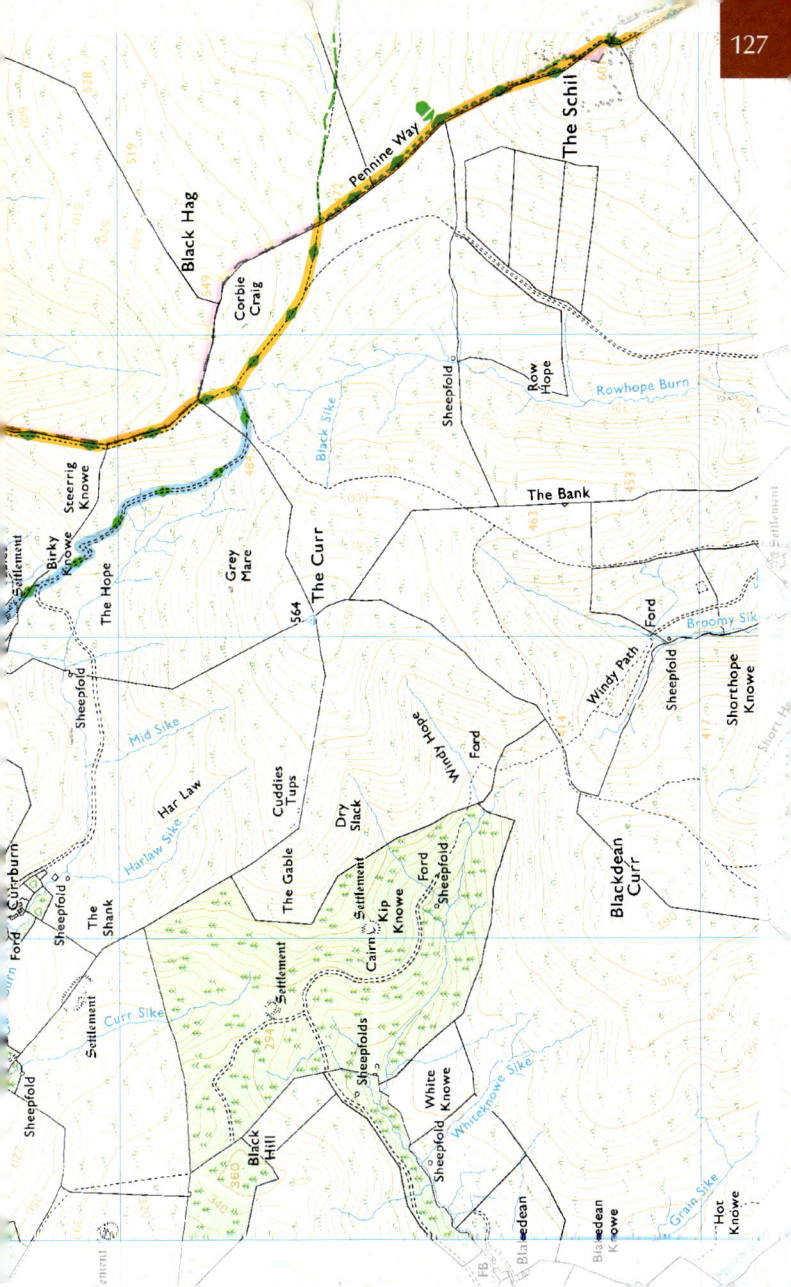

128

Name Kirk Yetholm to Clennell Street
Start The Green, Kirk Yetholm
Finish Clennell Street
Distance 22km (13.75 miles)
Time 7hr

LEGEND OF SYMBOLS USED ON ORDNANCE SURVEY 1:25,000 (EXPLORER) MAPPING

ROADS AND PATHS

Not necessarily rights of way

M1 or A6(M)	Motorway
A35	Dual carriageway
A30	Main road
B3074	Secondary road
	Narrow road with passing places
	Road under construction
	Road generally more than 4 m wide
	Road generally less than 4 m wide
	Other road, drive or track, fenced and unfenced
	Gradient: steeper than 20% (1 in 5); 14% (1 in 7) to 20% (1 in 5)
Ferry	Ferry; Ferry P – passenger only
	Path

- **S** Service Area
- **S** Service Area
- **7** Junction Number
- **T1** Toll road junction

RAILWAYS

- Multiple track / Single track — standard gauge
- Narrow gauge or Light rapid transit system (LRTS) and station
- Road over; road under; level crossing
- Cutting; tunnel; embankment
- Station, open to passengers; siding

PUBLIC RIGHTS OF WAY

- ---------- Footpath
- – – – – – Bridleway
- +++++ Byway open to all traffic
- – · – · – Restricted byway

The representation on this map of any other road, track or path is no evidence of the existence of a right of way

ARCHAEOLOGICAL AND HISTORICAL INFORMATION

✠	Site of antiquity	VILLA	Roman	✻	Visible earthwork
⚔ 1066	Site of battle (with date)	𝕮𝖆𝖘𝖙𝖑𝖊	Non-Roman		

Information provided by English Heritage for England and the Royal Commissions on the Ancient and Historical Monuments for Scotland and Wales

OTHER PUBLIC ACCESS

- • • •   Other routes with public access
- ◆ ◆ ◆   Recreational route
- ◆ ◆ ◆   National Trail   (symbol) Long Distance Route
- - - - -   Permissive footpath ⎫
- - - - -   Permissive bridleway ⎬ Footpaths and bridleways along which landowners have permitted public use but which are not rights of way. The agreement may be withdrawn
- • • •   Traffic-free cycle route
- 1 **1**   National cycle network route number – traffic free; on road

The exact nature of the rights on these routes and the existence of any restrictions may be checked with the local highway authority. Alignments are based on the best information available

ACCESS LAND

 Firing and test ranges in the area. Danger! Observe warning notices

 Access permitted within managed controls, for example, local byelaws. Visit **www.access.mod.uk** for information

England and Wales

 Access land boundary and tint

 Access land in wooded area

i   Access information point

Portrayal of access land on this map is intended as a guide to land which is normally available for access on foot, for example access land created under the Countryside and Rights of Way Act 2000, and land managed by the National Trust, Forestry Commission and Woodland Trust. Access for other activities may also exist. Some restrictions will apply; some land will be excluded from open access rights. The depiction of rights of access does not imply or express any warranty as to its accuracy or completeness. Observe local signs and follow the Countryside Code.
Visit **www.countrysideaccess.gov.uk** for up-to-date information

BOUNDARIES

- —+—+—   National
- — — —   County (England)
- — — —   Unitary Authority (UA), Metropolitan District (Met Dist), London Borough (LB) or District (Scotland & Wales are solely Unitary Authorities)
- · · · · ·   Civil Parish (CP) (England) or Community (C) (Wales)
- ———   National Park boundary

VEGETATION

Limits of vegetation are defined by positioning of symbols

- Coniferous trees
- Non-coniferous trees
- Coppice
- Orchard
- Scrub
- Bracken, heath or rough grassland
- Marsh, reeds or saltings

HEIGHTS AND NATURAL FEATURES

52 ·   Ground survey height
284   Air survey height

Surface heights are to the nearest metre above mean sea level. Where two heights are shown, the first height is to the base of the triangulation pillar and the second (in brackets) to the highest natural point of the hill

HEIGHTS AND NATURAL FEATURES (continued)

Vertical face/cliff

Loose rock | Boulders | Outcrop | Scree

Contours are at 5 or 10 metre vertical intervals

- Water
- Mud
- Sand; sand and shingle

SELECTED TOURIST AND LEISURE INFORMATION

- Building of historic interest
- Cadw
- Heritage centre
- Camp site
- Caravan site
- Camping and caravan site
- Castle / fort
- Cathedral / Abbey
- Craft centre
- Country park
- Cycle trail
- Mountain bike trail
- Cycle hire
- English Heritage
- Fishing
- Forestry Commission Visitor centre
- Garden / arboretum
- Golf course or links
- Historic Scotland
- Information centre, all year
- Information centre, seasonal
- Horse riding
- Museum
- National Park Visitor Centre (park logo) e.g. Yorkshire Dales
- Nature reserve
- National Trust
- Other tourist feature
- Parking
- Park and ride, all year
- Park and ride, seasonal
- Picnic site
- Preserved railway
- Public Convenience
- Public house/s
- Recreation / leisure / sports centre
- Roman site (Hadrian's Wall only)
- Slipway
- Telephone, emergency
- Telephone, public
- Telephone, roadside assistance
- Theme / pleasure park
- Viewpoint
- Visitor centre
- Walks / trails
- World Heritage site / area
- Water activites
- Boat trips
- Boat hire

(For complete legend and symbols, see any OS Explorer map)

NOTES

NOTES

THE PENNINE WAY

This map booklet accompanies the latest edition of Paddy Dillon's guidebook to walking the Pennine Way, described from south to north. The guidebook features annotated 1:100,000 mapping alongside a detailed step-by-step route description, full planning information and points of interest about local history, geography and wildlife.

The 'Hebden Bridge Loop' leads off-route into Hebden Bridge

OTHER CICERONE TRAIL GUIDES

 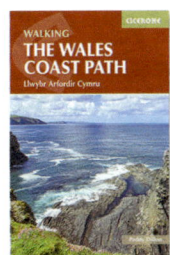 

Cicerone National Trails Guides
The South West Coast Path
The South Downs Way
The North Downs Way
The Ridgeway National Trail
The Thames Path
The Cotswold Way
The Peddars Way and
 Norfolk Coast Path
The Cleveland Way and
 the Yorkshire Wolds Way
Cycling the Pennine Bridleway
Hadrian's Wall Path
The Pembrokeshire Coast Path
Offa's Dyke Path
Glyndŵr's Way
The Southern Upland Way
The Speyside Way
The West Highland Way
The Great Glen Way

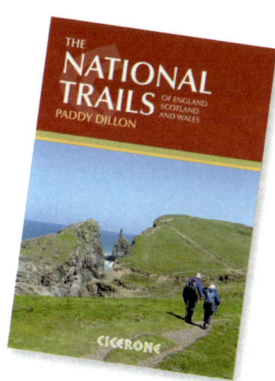

Visit our website for a full
list of Cicerone Trail Guides
www.cicerone.co.uk

CICERONE

Trust Cicerone to guide your next adventure, wherever it may be around the world...

Discover guides for hiking, mountain walking, backpacking, trekking, trail running, cycling and mountain biking, ski touring, climbing and scrambling in Britain, Europe and worldwide.

Connect with Cicerone online and find inspiration.

- buy books and ebooks
- articles, advice and trip reports
- GPX files and updates
- regular newsletter

cicerone.co.uk